The Omnipowerful Brand

The
Omnipowerful
Brand

America's #1 Brand Specialist
Shares His Secrets for
Catapulting Your Brand
to Marketing Stardom

Frank Delano

AMACOM
American Management Association

New York • Atlanta • Boston • Chicago • Kansas City • San Francisco • Washington, D.C.
Brussels • Mexico City • Tokyo • Toronto

This publication is designed to provide accurate and
authoritative information in regard to the subject matter
covered. It is sold with the understanding that the publisher
is not engaged in rendering legal, accounting, or other
professional service. If legal advice or other expert assistance
is required, the services of a competent professional person
should be sought.

Library of Congress Cataloging-in-Publication Data

Delano, Frank.
    The omnipowerful brand : America's #1 brand specialist shares his
    secrets for catapulting your brand to marketing stardom / Frank
    Delano.
        p.   cm.
    Includes index.
    ISBN 0-8144-0459-6
        1. Advertising—Brand name products.   I. Title.
    HF6161.B4D45   1998
    659.1—dc21   98–20739
                                                                  CIP

Printing number

10   9   8   7   6   5   4   3   2   1

Contents

Acknowledgments

I want to give special thanks to Ellen Kadin, Senior Acquisitions Editor, and Hank Kennedy, Publisher, at AMACOM Books for believing in this book.

Then there is someone at AMACOM who made this book abundantly more readable than it otherwise might have been—Mike Sivilli, Associate Editor. It's amazing how a good editor can clarify an author's manuscript, search out facts, and add that element of literary polish to his written prose. Thanks, Mike.

Other notable contributors to this book at AMACOM Books include Lydia Lewis, Production Manager, and her staff. To all of them: Thank you.

The fuel that drives a person to write a full-length book is the product of a lifetime. In that sense, I owe much gratitude to those whom I regard as early mentors. First, my father Frank, who taught me the values of hard work and honesty through personal example. My mother Caroline, who gave her love, compassion, and commonsense wisdom when it was needed most in my life. Walter Beach Humphrey, my high school art teacher and a noted muralist. Walter shaped my early notions of striving for excellence in all creative endeavors. An exceptional human being, Walter truly personified the word *teacher*. Fanny Upham, my high school English teacher. She believed in my artistic ability and encouraged me to pursue a career in the creative arts. Fanny also provided the theme (Washington Irving's fictional characters) for a 27-foot mural that I painted under Walter's art direction and which I dedicated to New Rochelle High School's English Department.

Thank God for all those remarkable high school teachers out there who provide such inspiration and motivation to their students. Ken Hiebert, my professor of graphic design at the University of the Arts, Philadelphia. Ken opened my eyes to the world of visual design, and encouraged me to stick to the knitting that I knew best.

Another mentor was Walter Margulies, a co-founder of Lippincott & Margulies, considered by many to be the McKinsey of the corporate identity business. Walter was a teacher on the importance of approaching marketing, communications, and design with business-like statesmanship. Walter greatly elevated the profession of brand management and corporate identity design in America today.

But the person who did the most to shape my thinking on building the omnipowerful brand was Bijan Pakzad, the creator, CEO, and president of Bijan, Designer for Men. His Rodeo Drive and Fifth Avenue flagship stores, and the Bijan fragrances for women and men are known around the world. I recall many discussions with Bijan in the mid-1970s when he was developing his fragrance brands—my office at that time was a five-minute walk to his Beverly Hills store. Hands down, he is America's quintessential master at making brands look magical. In this book, I talk about building the brand by paying close attention to "the little touches that add up to a big brand statement." Bijan was my teacher on the importance of this brand strategy, and all I can say is: Thank you, Bijan.

While they are nameless to me, many thanks go to the men and women who created the most brilliant brand marketing and ad themes of this century. I am talking about the creative geniuses who came up with brand themes like *"Come see the softer side of Sears," "Just for the taste of it," "This Bud's for you," "The Museum Watch," "The ultimate driving machine,"* and *"Just do it";* brand images like the Coca-Cola polar bears, the Energizer pink bunny, and the Maytag repairman—The Loneliest Guy in America; and brand names like Beetle, Absolut, Obsession, Planet Hollywood, Ziploc, Walkman, and Pentium. These are the folks who have catapulted American brands to global marketing stardom. Without their contributions, this book could not have been written.

Companies hire us to educate them on how to build image power for their brands. In truth, we always learn something valuable about building brands from every client we serve. What I have learned from them has provided the blueprint for this book. I can only bow my head in gratitude to the big-league companies that have placed their billion-dollar flagship brands in my firm's hands.

Then there's Cosmos, my golden retriever and best buddy. He stayed at my side countless nights and into the wee hours of morning, often with his head resting on my foot, while I revised one draft of the manuscript after the other. Cosmos, you're the greatest!

The song title reads: "The Wind Beneath My Wings." The wind beneath my wings in writing this book was one exceptional and beautiful woman: Wanda Lang. Wanda's support and encouragement can never be repaid in my lifetime. Thanks, Wanda.

To all the people mentioned above, this book is dedicated to you.

Introduction

Every company dreams of having a brand that is cherished by consumers worldwide. A brand that breaks through the barriers of more than 230 languages, countless cultures, different races, religions, and types of government. A brand that's never fenced in even when the company itself or its products are under pressure by the government, the news media, and consumer watchdog groups.

Now, imagine owning the rights to the worldwide-registered Coca-Cola brand. A brand that is the second most recognized word on planet Earth (the first is *hello*). A brand that has become so famous that millions of people from all walks of life are more than willing to pay a premium price for beer steins, alarm clocks, jackets, rhinestone-studded powder compacts and evening purses, among other personal and household items, that are adorned in one way or another with this commercial trademark. We're talking here about products that bear no resemblance to the dark-brown carbonated brew that made this brand an American icon.

But the king of soft drinks is not alone. Almost a skip and a hop away from The Coca-Cola Store on New York's Fifth Avenue and 56th Street, one of the world's most expensive strips of retail real estate, we find The Warner Bros. Studio Store (just expanded to nine shopping floors), The Disney Store, and Nike Town. They have all entered the fray to market such prized brands as Bugs Bunny, Mickey Mouse, Donald Duck, 101 Dalmatians, and Nike Air among a mind-boggling array of merchandise including fine art.

Just several blocks away from these new megabrand stores

are several "must see" restaurants for New York's tourists. They are marketing Planet Hollywood, Harley Davidson, Hard Rock Café, and Fashion Café as brands on merchandise like hats, sweatshirts, watches, boxer shorts, denim and leather jackets, backpacks, skinny tees, calendars, and other specialty items on sale to guests who want to take a piece of the brand home with them. Head south down to 49th Street and you'll find The Metropolitan Museum of Art Gift Shop; it's selling an array of products endorsed by the museum's brand name.

In Saturn's TV commercials, the spokesperson invites consumers to visit the Saturn manufacturing facility in Tennessee, and reminds them not to leave without shopping at The Saturn Store. Even the celebrated magician David Copperfield has now become a brand that transcends the world of illusion. Currently under construction in New York City is a $26 million David Copperfield "eatertainment" experience. More proof that the brand has no boundaries in the world of commercial enterprise except for the limitations of creative ideas.

Yes, the brand will be the name of the game far into the twenty-first century. Remember, it was those legendary corporate raiders of the 1970s who first educated Wall Street and the public to an understanding of what the "real prize" was in capturing a corporate giant. It wasn't the targeted company's manufacturing plants, R&D centers, sales force, distribution networks, management talent, or patents on new technology—it was the company's globally recognized brands.

Regardless of what you've heard or read, nothing is more important in building the brand than the selection of the brand's name. After all, if you don't start with a great brand name like Planet Hollywood, Sony's Walkman personal stereo, Nissan's Pathfinder, or Absolut Vodka, you're at a serious disadvantage in building what I call "The Omnipowerful Brand." Also keep this in mind: A compelling brand name can make a poor advertisement look good, but even the most compelling advertisement will stall if it features a poor brand name.

Thus, the first half of this book is focused on the seven proven principles and a proven process to find a great brand name—a brand name that launches the product, service, or business venture into the world's marketplace or replaces one that has proven to be a marketing dud. Where the product and its strategic image positioning are discussed in detail, it will serve to better your understanding of the brand name's selection. Other examples will help you to understand why the brand name selected proved to be a key factor in the product's success or its demise.

The conventional process used by companies in developing the brand's name is as outdated and unproductive as the horse and buggy. It's time for companies to board the Concorde—from the billion-dollar giants to the family-run business operations of every sort dotting the world's major markets, from tomorrow's start-up enterprises to Civil War-era companies like P&G. Simply put, any person involved in the creative or decision-making process of branding a corporation, product, service, or business venture will find this book to be essential reading.

The book's second half is devoted to what it takes to build a great brand name into the omnipowerful brand—a brand that transcends the very product that put it on the map. There are lessons from American companies on what works and what doesn't work in building and managing the brand. This sets the stage for the final chapter—"The Next Dimension in Power Brand Marketing."

This book provides examples from the marketplace where the omnipowerful brand has catapulted an above-average or me-too product into the realm of marketing stardom. It also offers many *powerbat** marketing ideas that any company regardless of its size, geographical reach, or industry can put into action.

There are brand-building stories told for the first time in print. For instance, you'll learn how my firm, Delano & Young, developed some of the most memorable brand names of the past half century—like Nissan's celebrated Pathfinder sport-utility, Pfizer's blockbuster Zoloft antidepressant drug, Abbott/Ross's globally marketed Survanta prenatal drug, Polaroid's

---

*The term *powerbat* refers to anything that exceeds someone's expectation such as hitting a home run with the bases loaded.

Captiva camera, GMC's Yukon luxury sport-utility, Oldsmobile's all-new Intrigue sports sedan, and Primerica financial
services. And you'll learn why the code name Taurus* was
selected for the branding of Ford's revolutionary-designed cars
and the role we played.

And for the first time ever in print, I reveal the finalist and
runner-up names that we created for the branding of major
products. Some of these names remain legally available today
for the branding of new products.

Here is one comment intended to help you through the
pages ahead: For simplicity's sake, the term *brand name* mentioned throughout this book in a general sense encompasses
the corporate, product, service, and business operation name.
And the term *product* used in a general sense refers not only
to the product itself but also to the corporation's service or
business operation.

---

*The author's firm advised Ford to adopt the code name Taurus for its
revolutionary-designed sedans and wagons in 1982.

Part One

In Pursuit of a Great Brand Name

1

A Brand Name
With No Boundaries

A brand name is no longer shackled to the product that made
it famous. It's a *free agent,* capable of being marketed on a
broad range of products that bear no resemblance to the original product. Yes, this may not be news to companies like Calvin Klein and Ralph Lauren, which have learned that their
fragrance brands like Polo and Eternity are more powerful
than the scents themselves. But it may be the best news ever
for thousands of other companies in mostly nonglamorous
businesses which never imagined that they could catapult
their brands to global marketing stardom. For these companies, this is the next dimension in power brand marketing for
the twenty-first century. And it's happening here in America
today thanks to such innovative marketers as Disney, Warner
Bros., Coca-Cola, Nike, Planet Hollywood, and Saturn, among
others.

The barriers have come down. The face of brand marketing is about to change big time, poised to take a giant leap
that's never been seen before in American business history.
Any company, regardless of the industry it's in, can make its
prized brands transcend the product. The secret to doing this
is finding ways to transform the brand's name into a tangible
asset that consumers want to own. The newest brand image-
building vehicle on the horizon is the company-owned brand
store.

I envision that by the year 2001 these megabrand stores

will pop up in the most unlikely places. The experience for consumers will be like shopping at Nike Town New York today.

Take New York's Franklin Delano Roosevelt midtown postal office on 54th Street and Third Avenue, just blocks away from my office. This two-story building's interior could easily be transformed into a megabrand U.S. Postal Store. If Warner Bros. Studio Store can market its globally recognized brand names like Bugs Bunny and Road Runner on a mind-boggling array of merchandise and fine art, just imagine the stockpile of famous brand-name images that the United States Postal Service has in its marketing war chest dating back to our country's independence from England. Recent examples of eminently marketable items include images of Marilyn, Elvis, and Count Basie. Even Ford's Mustang will appear on a new postal stamp in 1998 according to the U.S. Postal Service. With the right retail marketing environment and merchandise, this postal complex and dozens of others like it throughout the country could rival The Disney Store on Fifth Avenue by becoming a fun place for the public to shop for postage stamps, poster blowups of the artwork embodied on these stamps, and different-size packages in which to mail their holiday gifts.

I can also visualize The GM Store in the GM building on Fifth Avenue and 58th Street, just one block north of The Warner Bros. Store. It could market its brands like Corvette, Blazer, Seville, and Yukon on casual clothing, home and away-from-the-home merchandise, toys, and collectible art. The toys themselves could rival the F.A.O. Schwarz store in the GM building. Yukon camping gear, backpacks, parkas, sweaters, and footwear, natural line extensions of this GMC 4×4 utility vehicle built for exploring the outdoors, could outdo the Eddie Bauer store across the street. Disney's studio-signed copies of the original hand-painted cels used to make its animated movies would pale by comparison with the conceptual drawings, full-colored renderings, and three-dimensional models of GM's division cars and futuristic prototypes. The product design history dates back to 1897, with the Olds Curved Dash, America's first mass-produced automobile.

Manufacturers who assume that their boundaries in marketing have been set by traditional practices in their industry could be the big winners. Pharmaceutical houses have powerful brand names that could transcend the product. Visualize a warm-up suit with "Prozac Keeps Me Going" emblazoned in a rainbow of colors on the front. And what dog owner would pass up buying a doggy winter jacket at his veterinarian's mini-brand name store with the line "I Stopped Biting Now That I'm on Prozac"? Keep in mind that Prozac is now being prescribed by veterinarians for dogs with behavioral problems.

Then there's Viagra (pronounced like Niagra Falls), the impotence pill from Pfizer, Inc. In just one month following its availability in the United States (April 1998), Viagra, according to a May 7, 1998 article in *The Wall Street Journal,* has added a new dimension to the bedroom and become part of the nation's vernacular. The possibilities of marketing and licensing the name Viagra on just about everything that connotes resurrection, jump-starts, vim, and value is mind-boggling. One thing is for sure, the trademark law firms that Pfizer will need to hire to police its Viagra trademark worldwide stand to earn tens of millions of dollars.

Companies that want to reap the benefits of the new dimension in brand name marketing must have the "Omnipowerful Brand Name." And the first half of this book reveals the seven proven principles of branding and a step-by-step proven process toward finding it.

I've coined another term that also makes its debut in this book—the "Misery Name." This is the phonetically imperfect or inappropriate image name. Thousands of good to excellent products in all categories have been branded with the misery name. Eventually, it either chokes the product to death or keeps it from achieving its true sales potential. Brand names that drag the product down have no chance of becoming free agents.

For example, I can't imagine American consumers standing in line to enter The Hyundai Store to buy household items that are emblazoned with the name Hyundai or brands like Tiburon, Sonata, Elantra, and Accent. Yet this could become a reality if the Asian automaker's nameplate and its car model names were changed to omnipowerful brand names.

Want proof that products branded with the misery name can hurt sales? Well, in late February 1998, Hyundai announced that it was cutting its automotive production by a whopping 60 percent owing to weak sales in the United States. The people responsible for developing and approving Hyundai's brands and advertising should be assigned to other duties—they just don't get it.

If your company wants to build a brand name with no boundaries, keep these two thoughts in mind:

1. Despite the high odds (there are now 2.4 million U.S. registered trademarks), it's still possible to find the omnipowerful brand name.

2. Never underestimate the marketing clout that the omnipowerful brand name can give to a product that has the potential to enter the realm of marketing stardom. It can make the trip to the top a lot faster and far less costly in terms of advertising and marketing support.

2

The Current Process

Soon after word got around among the marketing staffs of Detroit's Big Three auto makers that the Delano firm had named Nissan's Pathfinder and GMC's Yukon and had advised Ford on the naming of its best-selling Taurus sedans and wagons, I got a call from a product manager at one of the car companies' divisions. His initial questions were typical: How much do you charge to name a new car and how long does the process take? I told him that our creative fee was $125,000 and the project could be completed in five to six weeks. He asked me to send him a written proposal via overnight delivery, which we did.

An Outdated and Unproductive Approach

About a week later, I was invited to the company's headquarters to make a presentation to the marketing staff on the Delano firm's naming capabilities. I felt that the meeting went well and that we had a good chance of getting this project. The next day back in my office, the product manager called. In an excited voice, he told me that the strategic marketing manager had selected our firm for name development. He asked if I would be willing to catch a flight that evening in order to attend a special new product briefing session the next morning at the company's Proving Grounds, for which the auto maker would pay us $5,000 for the one-day consulting time. "Yes," I

7

answered, assuming that the big project would follow after this kickoff session.

Entering the building's large presentation room the next day, I found myself in the company of some thirty-five people. They included the automaker's marketing and new product staff, engineering, product design, and manufacturing managers, and what looked like the advertising agency's entire account team. I couldn't help but notice poster-size sheets displayed on one wall with a list of names headed Car Name Candidates. I took my seat and for the next two hours an instructor led the all-male group through a creative thinking exercise on "What are things that can be divided?" Well, I learned that everything can be divided, but I wondered what this exercise was leading to. I found out during a coffee break that it was a warm-up for the afternoon session in which all the participants would either agree on a name from the candidates developed by the auto maker's marketing staff or brainstorm names for the new car. The goal was to have a car name decision by the late afternoon. I felt that I had been duped big time.

After lunch, I was asked to kick off the afternoon creative naming session. My first question was, "Are you serious about these candidate names displayed on the wall?" I looked at the director of strategic marketing, since he was running this meeting.

He replied, "Yes."

"You do recognize that many of these names like Sonata, Legacy, and Prelude are the names of existing cars and that others like Sensor and Crest are the names of major consumer products? Did you research these names for their legal availability?" I asked.

There was total silence.

"What is the essence, uniqueness, or spirit of this new car line?" I got no response. "What is the target buyer's motivation for owning this new car?" Not a voice spoke up. "Well then, what makes this new car different from the import cars or other domestic-built cars in the same price range?" Finally, a response!

"The new car is built on the same platform as other competing division models. Our job is to put the exterior and interior on this vehicle," answered the marketing executive, his face revealing more than a hint of embarrassment. "We brought you in today to help us name this vehicle, not to critique our creative process."

"How can you seriously consider any name without first identifying the product's essence—the reason why your division is bringing this new product into the marketplace?" I countered. For the next hour, I listened as people in the room blurted out one ridiculous name idea after another, names like Shogun, Flintstone, Crusader, and Carman. When I thought I had seen and heard it all, someone suggested the name John Wayne. For the next hour of this session, the names of male actors like Clint Eastwood and Humphrey Bogart were being given serious consideration. The brainstorming effort was clearly not focused on the product and I felt it was imperative to try to get things back on track. "Why not spend the remaining time left on defining the product's essence?"

"Essence! That's a good name," said the marketing leader with a grin like the mouse who had found the cheese. He wrote this word on one of the wall sheets and underscored it in red. "He's not serious about calling this new car Essence," I said to myself, "or is he?"

Aboard a flight back to New York that evening, I estimated the car company's division had invested close to six figures to bring this group together for one full day to name a car. But what stood out most in my mind was that a legendary division of one of America's biggest manufacturers and marketers of automobiles hadn't defined a proven process for product brand naming and had no understanding of the guiding principles in the development of the all-powerful brand name.

A year later, I saw a commercial on TV announcing the new car with the theme line "The Essence of _____." This vehicle was far from "the essence of excellence in luxury family transportation." Like most products whose advertising overpromises what the product can deliver, the car bombed soon after its introduction. Where had the auto maker's division gone wrong?

- It had squandered its budget for brand name creation on a brainstorming session without realizing that this method has a 95 percent failure rate.

- It hadn't defined the product's positioning statement, image profile, or the buyer's motivation for owning the product, among other marketing issues guiding the name creation process.

- It relied on people—employees and its ad agency—with no hands-on experience in naming products and no real commitment to the challenge.

- Top management had not taken charge in the naming of this major product. Instead, the product's brand name development had been palmed off onto one individual who was not qualified for the task.*

As Thomas J. Peters and Robert Waterman, Jr., point out in *In Search of Excellence* (New York: Harper & Row, 1982), the term *new product manager* originated with Procter & Gamble. This person is depicted in numerous marketing books as a showman-like entrepreneur, someone who is unafraid to take on the upper ranks of management to successfully position the company's new product in the marketplace against all odds. In reality, he is often a field sales representative with no hands-on brand marketing experience who has been drafted into the corporate marketing staff. He got the job because his predecessor either left the company or moved up the ladder to become brand manager of an established product. The last thing this individual wants to do is to challenge his senior. A pharmaceutical brand naming project comes to mind.

It was early morning when I arrived at the company's U.S. headquarters. I anticipated spending a long day in discussions with the marketing staff, research analysts, clinicians, chemists, and finally the senior vice president of marketing. My firm was hired to name an oral antibiotic drug. The first person I was to meet with was an associate product manager in his mid-twenties.

He was a soft-spoken, cordial fellow of medium build

*It should be noted that the automaker's division today has a new brand management team in place.

with dark brown hair and eyes. Over coffee, I asked, "Who will I be meeting with today and what are their roles in this project?"

"Well," he gasped, "I'm the only one you'll be talking with. The senior marketing manager made it clear to me that it's my responsibility to come up with a name recommendation for this new antibiotic."

"We're not naming a jock strap here," I said, my voice rising a pitch higher. "This oral drug will be marketed worldwide and could eventually reach sales of $500 million yearly. Don't you think I should hear other views about this new oral antibiotic from the people who are going to sign off on the brand name?"

"They're all tied up in meetings today, so you're going to have to rely on my input," he answered.

"Are you confident that you can guide us in the right direction?" I asked.

"Yes, I attended a staff meeting on this product when I joined this group," he replied.

"How long have you been with the company?" I asked.

"Two years as a field sales rep, and this is my third week in product management," he answered.

His predicament was not new to me. A product manager is competing with other brand managers. If the product he's assigned to turns out to be a big marketing success, he's an instant hero and his senior may soon be reporting to him. A few days later I sent him a go-forward letter. It detailed our understanding of the product's positioning, what the goals of the project were, and the do's and don'ts in developing names, with a suggestion that he review our naming strategy with his seniors for their agreement. He had asked us to develop names that would help identify the drug's generic name.

As we neared completion of the project, I reviewed with him several of our best candidate names to get his reaction. He felt we were right on track. We confirmed a date for presenting our best five names and five runners-up to his marketing superiors at the company's headquarters.

Minutes before my presentation started, he came into the conference room and pulled me to the side. "I hope you've got names here that are six letters," he said. His facial expression was noticeably tense.

"There are two," I answered. "The others are five, seven, and eight letters."

"I just found out this morning from a brand manager that the senior vice president of marketing, who will be at this meeting, has a superstition about the number of letters in a brand name. It's got to be six."

Sure enough, a name with six letters was favored by the marketing chief.

Looking at his staff, he said, "The brand name shouldn't sound like the generic name—it should be totally different."

Months later, the vice president of marketing gave us a new creative budget to develop names not based on the drug's generic name. The associate product manager was no longer involved in the project. I learned later that he had left the company. In the end, a name that we developed in the first round of names was approved by management.

The lesson here is that a company must take a team approach in naming a major new product, and senior managers must be active participants on this team. Now, keep these thoughts in mind:

- Don't ask your ad agency to create product names unless it has a proven process to follow and is committed to achieving the omnipowerful brand name.
- Unless you have an electronic naming program with "intelligence," using a computer to generate names is a waste of company staff time and money.
- Market testing brand-name candidates is a waste of management time and money unless these names have been legally cleared for availability and the test itself is structured to get the right information.

Why Ad Agencies Often Fail at Brand Naming

A scenario similar to the following fictional one takes place every day in American advertising agencies. An account manager tells the creative staff that its biggest client, Burgermax, is launching a new theme burger and the agency has been asked by the client to submit a list of suggested names for the new product.

"I know you've been burning the midnight oil working on the new TV spot for Burgermax," he says in a sympathetic tone, "but if each of you could find some time today to come up with about ten name ideas, that will give me enough names to appease Burgermax's vice president of marketing." He passes out a fact sheet explaining the new burger's marketing twist to the art directors and copywriters.

What's wrong with this picture? For starters, the new product's brand name is being presented to the agency's creative staff as an unwanted stepchild, a nuisance to them and to the agency. Next, there is no serious commitment of time being allocated to brand name development. By the day's end, the account manager will have his list of some hundred name ideas to fax to the client. But, more than likely, the names generated will either be identical with or too similar to registered trademarks for food and beverage products or they'll be way off track from the new product's correct positioning stance.

Seldom does my firm get a naming project in which the company's advertising and PR agencies haven't had a first go at naming the product. To make sure that we're not covering the same ground, we ask to see the names developed by these outside sources. A quick review of these agencies' recommended names confirms a lighthearted and unfocused approach to naming what may well be their client's most important new product launch ever. While there are dozens of naming projects that I could cite examples from, nothing tops the absurd names an American-based ad agency proposed for the branding of a Japanese-made sedan and wagon line marketed in the United States some years ago. Keep in mind, these were name recommendations for a low-end priced, no-frills, straightforwardly designed compact family car. Jay Leno could have a field day with material like this.

The ad agency's off-the-wall car brand names included:

Igniter   A wonderful name to convey that when you turn the ignition key, the vehicle explodes.

Fintex   What the hell is a "fintex?" It sounds like a woman's sanitary napkin.

Flasher   This car obviously comes with a raincoat.

Moonduster   What good is a family car if it doesn't dust the moon?

Sonicboom   You won't hear the engine running when you're inside the car because you may never hear again after the engine fires up.

Torch   Here we go again—the car ignites into flames.

Godzilla   Imagine asking a parking attendant to treat your Godzilla with tender loving care.

Cassiopeia   Sounds like a terminal blood disease.

Clay   When you pay off the car loan, you get the metal body and engine.

Rex   A popular name for a German shepherd attack dog.

Shyhawke   A car named after a wild bird that's afraid to venture out.

Quaterfoil   Sounds like a car that can be submerged in water.

Terminator   Now here's a car name that should get some respect if you're driving along Webster Avenue in the South Bronx late at night.

Jet Liner   The ideal name for a compact family vehicle.

Presidential Line   Certainly denotes an entry-level, low-end-priced, no-frills car.

Aristocrat   C'mon, this is a car built for the common folk, not the Prince of Wales.

Shalom   This name would play well in the Bible Belt.

Bi-Trac   Implies that you can drive on both sides of the road with this car.

Adder   Sounds like "you gotta adda somma-thing to this car."

Scarab   Brings to mind a car crash that leaves the driver and passengers with scars and scabs.

The ad agency's car brand names that infringed on other famous registered trademarks included:

Stingray   Hey, that's Corvette's name and it's a GM registered trademark.

Luxus Hey, that sounds and looks a lot like the Lexus car name, and the name Lexus is a registered trademark owned by Toyota.

Electra Hey, this is Buick's top-of-the-line car model line name and a GM registered trademark.

Atlas Hey, this is a famous automotive tire brand name owned by Atlas Supply Company of Akron, Ohio, whose trademark registration dates back to 1931.

Starlite Hey, wasn't that the name of a Studebaker car line?

Quasar Hey, that's a famous brand name in consumer electronics, and cars have lots of electronic components in them.

Villager Hey, that's a Mercury car line name and it's been a Ford registered trademark since 1959.

Vantage Hey, that's a leading cigarette brand.

Marathon Hey, that's the name of Marathon Oil Company's automotive service stations.

Intruder Hey, my firm named the Suzuki Intruder motorcycle, and the name Intruder is a registered trademark owned by Suzuki Motor Corp. since 1986.

Century Hey, that's another Buick car name and it's a GM registered trademark dating back to 1972.

Galaxy Hey, the name Galaxie is owned by Ford; the Ford Galaxie was one of America's most popular cars in the 1960s and the trademark registration dates back to 1959.

Needless to say, the Japanese automaker's American marketing executives passed on all the names just cited for the same reasons I've noted. As a side note, the ad agency lost the account shortly after the car line was introduced.

If we look deeper, we may find the reasons ad agencies and their people are less than enthusiastic about creating brand names. First, an agency typically earns its money on the commission rates it receives from the advertiser's media costs. Creative services are expected to be performed in return for these commission fees, and that often means providing creative input on ancillary projects related to products, services, and business operations featured in TV commercials and print advertisements. So, understandably, there's no financial incentive for the agency to go all out on nonrevenue-producing client projects. Second, advertising people want to be associated with TV spots that win Clios (the equivalent of an Oscar in the motion picture industry). But saying I named this product and that product is not the way to climb the creative ladder in a major advertising firm.

Because many agencies get requests to develop new product or business names only on an infrequent basis—maybe once in any given year—there's no effort made by the agency to formulate a proven process for this specialized creative work. As a result, there are no guidelines for channeling creativity in productive directions; no image and functional naming criteria for measuring the appropriateness of the names developed; and no procedural knowledge about how to evaluate names for use and availability. For the client, it usually ends up being: "Is there any name on the agency's list that we can use both from a marketing and legal standpoint?" This is not how you develop the omnipowerful brand name, as you'll discover in Chapters 5 and 6 of this book.

Why Not to Rely on Computer-Generated Names

If you're computer-literate, you should be able to program your PC to run out on your laser printer every conceivable word citation built from the vowels and consonants you've selected. If you selected three vowels and four consonants, about four hours later you should have fifteen pounds of paper on your desk listing some 25,000 unknown citations and maybe twenty-five that you'll find in *Webster's*.

Now, if you were looking for a great consumer product name, what are your chances of finding it among these 25,000 mostly indiscernible words? The answer is: quite low. And if you found one that you did like, would you really want to brand your consumer product with a computer-generated word like Nexcoas or Nadibom?

Of course, you also have the option of purchasing a so-called naming software program that will cost between $200 and $1,000. These programs are essentially synonym finders in electronic form. Let's say you bought one and you're using it to find a new women's fragrance brand name that will express the idea of "fantasy." More than likely, such nouns as *delusion, aberration, horror, fear, nightmare, craziness,* and *screwball* will appear on your PC monitor because the program you purchased lacks the intelligence to eliminate negative or inappropriate image words. More appropriate image nouns like *dream, myth, legend,* or *mystery* may also appear on your monitor. However, your program doesn't know that these words are U.S. registered trademarks for toiletries and cosmetics because it lacks trademark searching intelligence. You'll also probably find a listing of nouns like *conceptualization, imagination, resourcefulness,* and *inventiveness* that are too unwieldy or strange for the branding of a women's fragrance or any other consumer product. Here again, your program lacks the intelligence to identify appropriate image words by a specified letter count or to find words starting with a preferred vowel or consonant, and so on.

Without basic intelligence built into your computer's naming software program, you'll soon realize that it's far more productive to refer to word reference books. Yet, if your company needs brand name ideas for a continuous flow of new products, services, and business ventures, developing a custom naming software program with intelligence makes good business sense (see "The NameVoyage Electronic Naming Process" in Chapter 3).

When Market Testing of Names Is a Waste of Time and Money

Call it asinine, total stupidity, a flagrant disregard for corporate expenditures, or anything else you want to label it. I am talking about corporate in-house marketing staffs who take proposed brand names into a costly market test before these names have been cleared for use and availability.

If this happened infrequently, it wouldn't be worth mentioning. The fact is, it is done more times than not by all companies, including the giants of industry. The corporate love affair with testing every marketing idea with consumers is part of the reason. But there are other reasons, too. Marketing staffs often assume that if they're testing five names, a majority of them should prove to be available. Others are simply unaware of the legal clearing process that must take place, never giving a thought to the fact that within a specific industry there can be tens of thousands of registered brand names and thousands more pending registration. Still others, who should know better, will bypass the legal clearing hurdle because it takes too long for the company's legal department to voice an opinion on name availability.

The cost of market testing names in several major cities can run from the mid- to high-five figures and well into six figures for national and international quantitative research findings. In view of these costs, corporate management should make it mandatory that no new product or business names be tested before they receive a preliminary green light from legal. At the same time, with easy access to domestic and international online trademark and trade name banks, corporate legal staffs should be able to make preliminary name availability evaluations within forty-eight hours or less. So, there should be no excuse for bypassing the name clearing process in the rush to get market research data.

3

A New Understanding: The Brand Name as King

Nothing is more important in a new brand's marketing strategy than the selection of the brand's name. Yes, you heard it right! It's more important than the brand's graphics, packaging design, advertising theme line and campaign, slogan, the brand's selling environment, and the brand's PR program. In fact, in many cases, the brand's name is even more important than the product itself, especially when it's a me-too product.

Take Pepsi-Cola. This globally marketed American brand icon is a copycat product in the truest sense. The product's formulation, taste, refreshment quality, fizzle, and visual appearance are so close to Coca-Cola's that it's virtually impossible for most cola soft drink enthusiasts to tell the two products apart in a blind taste test. Let's not forget, however, that Coke is the original dark-brown carbonated cola brew dating back to 1892. Pepsi's graphics, packaging, advertising themes and campaigns, and product spokespeople have all changed numerous times since World War II. In fact, after a total package redesign a few years ago, Pepsi-Cola announced that it would debut a new packaging design in 1998 to commemorate its centennial anniversary. But one thing hasn't changed—the Pepsi brand name. It's the glue that binds this brand together with hundreds of millions of loyal Pepsi and Diet Pepsi drinkers around the world.

Now, it should be obvious why the search for a great brand name assumes such importance in this book. For those corporate executives and entrepreneurs who doubt that the brand's name rules the marketing picture, consider these realities from the marketplace:

▪ *You cannot go forward with a new product launch or business venture without first having a name to brand that new product or company.* How can you develop a brand logo and packaging design, ad and PR campaigns, product brochures and announcements, and a myriad of other media items unless you have a brand name?

▪ *Most products come to our attention by word of mouth.* The brand's name is almost always the first element in the product's marketing picture to attract consumers' interest in the product.

▪ *Remove the brand name from 95 percent of the products sold in America and you'll have instant product anonymity.* Only about 5 percent of the nation's products would be identified by their graphics or packaging design in the absence of the product's brand name. Coca-Cola's swirling white ribbon on a red background, the Betty Crocker spoon on the package, and Absolut Vodka's loglike bottle shape are three such exceptions.

A Wake-Up Call

If you have a new product or service in the development pipeline or a new business venture or merger on the drawing board, now is the time to name it and to secure a claim of ownership to the name. The following facts and trends are intended to sound a wake-up call to corporate America:

▪ A record 188,080 trademark applications were filed with the U.S. Patent and Trademark Office in the agency's fiscal 1997 year, as compared with 83,169 filed in 1989, the year before new relaxed trademark laws were passed by Congress, and 69,253 filed a decade earlier.* Only four out of ten appli-

---

*Information provided by the USP&TO's public affairs department.

cations filed in 1997 will be granted trademark registrations because of conflicts with trademarks already registered or pending registration.

▪ The number of trademark applications filed by both U.S. and foreign companies and individuals under the "Intent-to-Use" brand name in the U.S. marketplace is expected to soar to more than 400,000 by the year 2001. It's estimated that only two out of ten applications will be approved owing to trademark conflict issues. That's a sobering thought.

The Brand Name Today

The brand name is no longer just a "silent salesperson" that appears on the product or the product's packaging. Those platitudes we read in business journals and marketing books about the brand's image being the sum total of the product's name, graphics, package design, and advertising campaign are your father's thinking. I explain what the brand is all about in the second half of this book. However, in your pursuit of the omnipowerful brand name, it's important to keep these thoughts in mind:

- ▪ The corporate name is also the company's brand name and it should be managed as a brand, not as a corporate signature.
- ▪ The salesperson explaining the product to the potential buyer or user is the brand name.
- ▪ The guarantee or warranty behind the product is the brand name.
- ▪ The service support behind the product is the brand name.
- ▪ A new business venture is the brand name.
- ▪ A contractual handshake is the brand name.

The Name Team

Most companies, large and small, fail to recognize the value of organizing a name team to take full responsibility for the branding of the company's products. Those that do often put together a group that's unmanageably large or composed of the wrong people. A five-member team generally works best, and each member of such a team must be equal in rank to all other members regardless of his or her job position or status. Equally important, each must be an actual participant in the brand name creation process—doing research, performing preliminary availability and language checks of candidate names, and presenting name recommendations and findings to the other team members at each name review meeting.

In Search of That Elusive Word or Syllable

You need more than your brain's vocabulary power, *Webster's Dictionary,* and *Roget's Thesaurus* in the pursuit of the omni-powerful brand name. Searching for that elusive word or syllable to complete the brand name puzzle is part of the brand naming specialist's life. I walk several miles daily through Manhattan in the search for inspiration at book and record stores, apparel and jewelry boutiques, wine emporiums, perfume counters, and museums. Italian footwear makers, for example, love to brand their shoes, slippers, and boots with fanciful European-sounding names like Palladio, Altima, and Calebre. Of all the places I have sought out, however, none is more offbeat than a Catholic seminary.

Birth of a Lifesaving Brand

My firm's mission was to name a new lifesaving surfactant drug developed by Abbott/Ross Laboratories, based in Columbus, Ohio. Surfactant is an emulsifying—whitish sudsy-looking—chemical produced in the late stages of gestation both in humans and animals. It prevents the tendency of lung tissue to collapse spontaneously on expiration.

Thanks to Abbott/Ross's new drug, it's now widely known among the world's medical professionals that a lack of surfactant is the primary cause of respiratory distress syndrome (RDS) in newborns. A single and painless oral dose of purified extract of surfactant obtained from bovine (cow) lung immediately improves the infant's lung function, lessens the need for high concentrations of oxygen, and lowers pulmonary airway pressure. Prior to this drug's development, some eight thousand premature infants died each year in the United States from a lack of naturally-produced oxygen, and thousands suffered brain damage or blindness from excessive exposure to administered oxygen. Undoubtedly, Abbott/Ross's surfactant compound ranks among the most valuable medicines developed in this century.

I had the good fortune of working with Abbott/Ross's Ron Bernard, director of strategic marketing planning. Unlike many top marketing officers I've come to know in the brand management and naming business, Bernard didn't hire us; rather, he rolled up his sleeves and worked with us in a team effort. If this one statement helps to change the way senior marketing executives work with brand specialists, their investment in this book will have been returned a thousandfold.

This wasn't the only product we were naming for Abbott/ Ross; there were four others. But I got the immediate sense after talking to Bernard that the surfactant drug was *his* child and he was determined to see it succeed.

Bernard arranged for our team to interview some twenty-five people who were, or would be, involved in the surfactant's research and product development, its manufacturing, marketing and sales, and distribution. Lengthy discussions were also held with Bernard's seniors, including the president of the Ross division.

We also talked to neonatologists, pediatricians, obstetricians, gynecologists, and other medical professionals working in hospital neonatal units to gain their perceptions of the therapeutic efficacy and safety of surfactant.

These fact-finding sessions led to two conclusions: Abbott/Ross's pulmonary surfactant drug would have to be viewed by neonatologists as clinically proven and safe for newborns in that it had no adverse side effects; and it would need to be positioned as a medicine valuable to humanity. Because Abbott/Ross would be the first to launch a surfactant medicine, there was an opportunity to create a distinctive brand name that would be remembered by specialists in the premature infant health care field.

The parents of premature infants were also an important factor in the acceptance of this new medicine. I realized early on that the perfect brand name would convey warmth and humanism and speak to the wonderful lifesaving properties of this drug. Bernard agreed that a strong chemical-sounding name like Axotax would only add to the mother's anxieties about her tiny newborn's chance of survival.

I like creating names in the late evening and early morning hours. On this particular evening, I was looking over my notes from various Abbott/Ross interview sessions. My eye caught a comment made by the senior marketing chief: "Surfactant is the 'breath of life' to the premature baby."

"Where did I hear that before?" I asked. "Of course, it's in the Book of Genesis: 'God blew into Adam's nostrils and gave him the breath of life.' " As the normal workday started, I wondered if this phrase, "breath of life," appeared in the Bible as one word in all major foreign languages dating back to the fifteenth century, when the printing press was invented. Logic told me that any earlier single-word translations into Arabic, Armenian, or Greek would not have the right phonetic sound. I called a Catholic seminary in Manhattan in the hope of finding the answer.

Going from one department to another, I finally spoke to a nun who worked in her order's library. I told her what I was after. She was amazed that anyone could make a living naming products. Happy to assist me, she went right to work.

Late that afternoon the sister called. The word I was hoping to hear was in French—*vivant, vi* meaning "life" and *vant* meaning "to breathe." I already had the first piece of the puzzle with the prefix *sur* from *surfactant*. It was obvious that the word *survivant* had an awkward phonetic sound. But *survant*, meaning "surfactant for breath," was almost there. Ending the word with the letter *a* added the warmth and humanism I was after. Thus, Survanta was coined.

This distinctive and memorable brand name has helped to make Abbott/Ross's pulmonary surfactant drug a marketing success story. But the credit must be shared with Ron Bernard and all the other people at Abbott/Ross who provided the insight and inspiration to help us develop the omnipowerful brand name.

The Trademark Attorney

One has to respect the responsibility that a company's trademark attorney takes on when he gives management his official approval on a major new product, service, or business merger name. If he has made the wrong call, the company risks being sued for trademark or trade name infringement. And if the plaintiff wins in or out of court, the cost to remove the name from the marketplace and to install a new brand moniker can easily run into millions of dollars, and that's not including damages paid to the suing party. Then, if that's not enough, there's the public embarrassment to the company's management for having made such a business blunder.

The victory does not always go to the Goliath; witness Goodyear's encounter with a small Colorado tire company years ago. A Denver federal district court ruled that Big O Tire Dealers had the rights under common law to a snowmobile track branded Big Foot. The court assessed damages of about $17 million against the world's largest tire manufacturer in connection with its introduction of the Big Foot radial brand name.

One of the hardest calls a trademark attorney has to make is when the name is a dictionary word related to the company's industry or the product itself. For instance, calling a new restaurant chain or line of prepared foods Escoffier or a brand of hunting knives Excalibur will only increase the odds of a trademark or trade name confrontation.

When the Helmsley hotel chain announced the grand opening of the posh Palace in New York City's midtown district, it was promptly sued by the owner of a small hotel in lower Manhattan having the same name. Helmsley had already invested a considerable sum in having the Palace brand name inscribed, etched, embossed, printed, or woven on thousands of items. But the chain was forced to modify the name of its chic Madison Avenue hostelry to the Helmsley Palace.

The trademark attorney has assumed the unenviable role of passing judgment on the top names that the company's marketing, sales, or advertising executives have recommended to management. When his or her opinions on these names are not favorable, these executives, understandably, are tempted to vent their anger on the attorney by accusing him of being unreasonable or "Chicken Little." You'll be better off, however, if you treat your company's trademark counsel in a professional manner and request that he put his opinions in writing, citing the specific trademark or trade name conflicts that he foresees. Remember, you'll have to deal with the same attorney on the next naming project and you'll probably never have a better friend in a large corporation since his call on a name's availability may well save your hide, too.

In most medium-size and large companies, the trademark attorney will ordinarily agree to have an independent trademark attorney firm conduct its own search of a name in question and submit its opinion on the name's availability. If the outside firm takes the position that the name appears to be available and will likely be granted a U.S. trademark registration, then it obviously becomes a business decision to go forward with that name.

Bring in the company's internal or external trademark attorney at the start (not the end) of the brand name creation process. The procedure we follow at my firm is to have the company's trademark attorney clear finalist and runner-up names for domestic and international use before these names are reviewed with management. *For God's sake, never present finalist names to senior management before they have been evaluated for their use and availability by a competent trademark attorney.*

Establishing a good working relationship with the company's trademark attorney doesn't mean that you should be intimidated by his role in the brand name selection process. When his opinions on name availability are completely off-the-wall, be prepared to fight for what you believe is the best name for the product. A brand naming project for Clairol comes to mind.

Worth the Trouble for Clairol

In 1990, Clairol's then vice president of new products, Nancy Flinn, hired my firm at a creative fee in the high five figures to name a new permanent no-mix hair color. Flinn made a point of telling me three times that this was the highest fee Clairol had ever paid for name creation. I replied, "When you enter into the tiger's den, you've got to be well compensated." She grinned, knowing very well that in the beauty products business you could be loved today and devoured tomorrow if a major new product bombs.

Priced at around ten dollars, Clairol's product would be the most expensive retail hair color ever launched. The price was justified because the color was premixed and ready to apply from an aerosol container. The target buyers were upscale women willing to pay a few dollars more for these innovative product features.

L'Oréal's Preference, priced at eight dollars per single application, was the competition to beat. The brand Preference was well established as a premium hair color with its brilliant advertising line, "It's expensive, but I'm worth it." The challenge was to come up with a name that said, "This product is more expensive than Preference, but I'm worth it."

Reviewing the names we created over a four-week period, I rated Affluence one of the best. It spoke to confident, sophisticated women who had the means to enjoy the best permanent hair color available. The qualitative market test we conducted with some thirty professional women who colored their own hair confirmed my conviction. This name and other finalists were evaluated for their legal availability.

This included computer database searches of some 1.8 million registered trademarks and pending registrations in all international classes as well as a review of trademark applications filed with the U.S. Patent and Trademark Office. Before we showed our best names to Flinn, a no-nonsense executive in her late forties or early fifties, we wanted to be 95 percent sure that they were clear for use as a hair color brand name and were likely to be granted U.S. trademark registration. A creative firm that promises to deliver names that are 100 percent legally available is either inexperienced or lying to its client.

My presentation of our finalist names to Flinn and her staff came off with flying colors. I left Clairol's headquarters on Park Avenue puffed up with pride. But that balloon burst days later with the news that a Clairol attorney had ruled Affluence and our other top names unavailable for a hair color marketed in the United States. When you know you've got the omnipowerful brand name for a major product, you can't walk away that easily. So, I called Flinn.

"Forget it, Frank," said Flinn. "At Bristol-Myers [the parent of Clairol], the attorney has the last word." Bristol-Myers since merged with Squibb to form Bristol-Myers Squibb.

"Ask the attorney to call me. I think you and I have the right to know what is the cloud hanging over Affluence. I can tell you that we did a thorough search and found no clouds." The tone of my voice convinced her that we had a chance of prevailing.

My conversation with the attorney confirmed what I had surmised. He was young, had little experience in trademark law, and was going to play it ultrasafe since it was his head on the block. God only knows how many great brand names have been killed since the turn of this century because the trademark attorney put his home mortgage payment ahead of the company's best interest.

I spoke with the attorney and learned that the cloud he saw was a trademark application for the name Affluent, limited to rubberized underwear for bladder control.

"Listen," I said, "these names are not spelled the same and the name Clairol will always be linked with Affluence. The products are in totally different classes—one is a hair color and the other is a hygiene-related undergarment. The products will never appear together in the same selling environment, and do you actually believe consumers would confuse an unknown producer of rubberized underwear with the world's largest marketer of hair color?" He knew I was right, but he refused to change his position, probably out of embarrassment.

Fortunately, the chief legal counsel at Bristol-Myers, after hearing the facts, reversed the junior attorney's decision. Affluence was granted a U.S. trademark registration in 1991 for Clairol's beauty products.

When a Name Is Dropped

Even a most experienced, competent, and open-minded trademark attorney, like Ken Enborg at General Motors, must rely on his gut feeling about the availability of a proposed name for the branding of a product, service, or business operation. When my firm was developing brand name recommendations for GM Oldsmobile's new flagship sedan (Aurora), one of our finalists was Contoura, built from the word *contour.* Oldsmobile's marketing staff gave this name high marks because it spoke to the car's sleek design styling. And the preliminary trademark and trade name searches we conducted supported our conviction that the name Contoura was available in the states and would likely receive a U.S. trademark registration in Class 12-Automobiles. However, when Enborg conducted an international trademark search of the name Contoura, he found a Canadian registration for the name Contouro, and the company that owned it happened to manufacture automobile replacement seat covers in North America.

Enborg advised Oldsmobile's management to consider other names we had developed that would not provoke conflict with an existing or pending registered trademark in the United States, Canada, and Mexico. Management heeded his counsel and the name Contoura was removed as a finalist. Now, here's the kicker: Ford launched the Contour four-door sedan a year later and, to the best of my knowledge, the name was never challenged.

What's the lesson here? You must respect dark and ominous-looking clouds that loom over a proposed brand name. On the other hand, you cannot run scared every time you find a grayish-looking cloud in the sky.

The Need for a Proven Process in Brand Naming

My firm takes a two-pronged approach to creating brand names. We rely on the talent and skill of our people and on our firm's proprietary NameVoyage electronic naming process. Regardless of the approach we take, success is based on following the seven proven principles and the proven process detailed in this book.

Within most companies there are people who have a flair for inventing words, and they are not necessarily found in the marketing or creative departments. While they may not rank among this country's top brand name specialists, they have a good chance of finding the product's omnipowerful brand name if they learn basic skills in naming products and follow the methodology outlined here. Often people with solid literary backgrounds have a difficult time in creating successful brand names for the mass market, but there's a solution to every obstacle.

The NameVoyage Electronic Naming Process

NameVoyage is the world's only electronic naming process with intelligence. Using it is like traveling aboard the Concorde as compared with making do with the horse-and-buggy conventional brainstorming process used by advertising agencies and corporate in-house marketing staffs to develop name recommendations. The intent here is to provide readers with the advances that have been made at the top end of the brand naming and identity business over the past decade.

When you're at the creation station of this million-dollar (estimated market value) state-of-the-art interactive naming and identity system, you're in command of a vast electronic library comprising more than 2.5 million word citations, both real and created, and thousands of video images.

Watching hundreds and sometimes thousands of words flash across the giant NameVoyage screen is like taking a voyage through a galaxy of names. Hence the name NameVoyage.

You have the power, with the click of a handset, to capture any one of them for the branding of a product, service, or business venture. I also designed NameVoyage to create new names and images for people in all professions, as well as for their prized possessions like yachts, racehorses, and so on.

Obviously, I can't give you a demonstration of this naming and identity process in print or reveal its proprietary electronic architectural design. What I will tell you is how I used NameVoyage to create the identity for a character in a new movie made for television, and that should give you an idea of NameVoyage's capabilities.

The character in the TV pilot is a stunning actress and model in her mid-thirties who is out to seduce a celebrated novelist who's currently writing a book about a man's quest to win a beautiful, sexually provocative woman. In one of her three seductive roles, she's a dancer at a Los Angeles Latin nightclub. My objective for this role was to create a name not typical of a woman with hot Latin blood running through her veins like Rosa Carlos.

Working late again, I called up a provocative photo image of the actress on the NameVoyage screen while listening to Luis Miguel's CD "Secondo Romance." I defined the character's profile in five key image words and entered them on the screen: She's supreme, powerful, exciting, controlling, and intimidating.

Next, using voice activation, I instructed NameVoyage to search for words that were associated with these image qualities. Within seconds, words flashed on the screen across the life-size photo image of the actress in a black sequined silk short dress with spaghetti straps; hot black hose; black silk spiked heels with red sparkles; gold Paloma Picasso "Kiss" earrings and matching necklace, and a red silk heart-shaped gold chain bag over her shoulder.

When the words stopped, I zoomed in on the word *dominance*. Then I asked NameVoyage to search through its library of created words to find those that started with the letters *D-O-M-I-N*. Again, as words flashed across the screen, I highlighted the word *dominia*. Turning to my assistant, I said, "That's her first name; now we've got to find her last name."

"Frank," she asked, "what type of last name goes with Dominia?"

"What we need is a name that reveals the complexity and mystery of this exciting woman. A real word. One that evokes a temptress who's well aware that men find her captivating, alluring, and sensual.

"It has to convey femininity and sensuality. A short word—no more than four letters and one syllable to contrast in look and sound with her first name. Yet there's got to be a phonetic marriage between the first and last names—as if they were destined to be together," I answered.

"How did you learn to create names?" she asked.

"When a great chef creates a dish, everything speaks to him—the smell, look, texture of the food, and even the sound of it sizzling in a hot skillet. That's the kind of sensitivity and awareness that one must develop in this business." I paused momentarily, then continued, "Did you know that Shakespeare coined over 1,700 words in his lifetime?"

"No, I had no idea," she replied. "Give me an example."

"*Monumental* is one of his fifty-dollar words," I said. "It used to be a fifty-cent word when I was in grade school, but I've adjusted the amount to reflect today's cost of living in New York City." She laughed. I continued, "Well, before Shakespeare gave us that adjective, it took several less expensive adjectives like *big, grand,* and *great* to convey the same thought. What images come to mind when you hear the word *monumental?*"

Her silence lasted but a few seconds; then she blurted out, "The Golden Gate Bridge in San Francisco . . . the Bible . . . and . . ."

"Great, enough!" I interrupted. "You perceived the single images that Shakespeare would have wanted you to recall if he were standing here today. The next time you see this Shakespearean word remember that *mon* means 'single' and *mental* means 'relating to emotions of the mind.' So, these two words joined together mean 'a single image fixed forever in one's mind.' Even the *u* bridge letter was a masterful touch because this long-sounding vowel imparts a greater sense of importance to the word's meaning. What I just told you is not found in *Webster's* or any other book."

With this in mind, I instructed NameVoyage to identify one-syllable words in English comprising no more than four letters that conveyed the words *sensuality* and *femininity.* As the words flashed on the screen, I selected the word *lace.* DOMINIA LACE was now emblazoned on the screen. Next, I created a *SPIN* magazine cover layout on the screen, superimposed a full-color head shot of the actress on the cover, and added this headline in a red Times Roman boldface: "SEXY DOMINIA LACE Talks About Her Love for Latin Dancing and Her New Love."

Then I asked NameVoyage to search its domestic and international databases of trademarks, trade names, common law marks, and celebrity names to confirm the availability and use of this name. About five minutes later, the message "No identical or almost identical hits found" appeared on the screen.

"Meet Ms. Dominia Lace," I said to my assistant.

Here's what gives NameVoyage the advantage in building the omnipowerful brand name:

- It searches through major languages to find words we often overlook that have an image association with the key image profile words entered into the system. Because these words are not synonyms of the profile words, they have a greater chance of being available for the branding of globally marketed products. Look up the word *femininity* in a synonym reference book and you will not find the word *lace.* Yet the word *lace* certainly captures the essence of femininity.

- It can search through names in five major languages to identify any negative or inappropriate meanings or connotations, literal or slang.

- If you have a prefix, root, or suffix in mind to build a name from, NameVoyage can complete the word to the precise number of letters and phonetic sound you desire.

- It can identify words by their sexual profile.

4

Secrets to Naming Products and Companies

Most that's been written about the fine points of creating a brand name not only can be tossed out, it should be.

—Frank Delano

Little has changed in the creative business since Michelangelo labored eighteen-hour days trying to meet the insatiable demands of his studio's clientele. In fact, the great Renaissance master never did meet his contractual obligation to Pope Julius II. He was to have completed a colossal two-story marble burial tomb adorned with forty larger-than-life carved marble figures for this tough, no-nonsense ruler of the Papal See. When Julius died, the sculptor thought that the worst business deal he had ever entered into was *finito*. However, he spent his remaining days fighting legal actions brought by Julius's nephews. Many people are unaware of the commissioner of this work, but few have forgotten some of the masterpieces that were completed: Michelangelo's *Moses* and his *Rebellious Slaves* and *Dying Slaves,* to mention three examples.

The Passion, Hard Work, and Visualization It Takes

The tools of the modern-day creator have changed drastically since the early sixteenth century. We have three-dimensional computer modeling, interactive media, desktop publishing, virtual reality, and the Internet. But the creation of great works still takes a passion for the calling and hard work; this includes the pursuit of the omnipowerful brand name.

Hemingway struggled to come up with the book title *For Whom the Bell Tolls.* The famed novelist had five words with nineteen characters to get our attention. Imagine if he had been faced with the challenge of finding one word with no more than two syllables and seven letters to communicate the essence of his novel—a single word that has no geographical boundaries, no negative connotation in any foreign language, and doesn't infringe on someone else's domestic or foreign trademark. That's the formidable task presented to my firm when we're called upon by GM, Ford, Coca-Cola, Pfizer, Seagram, or Polaroid, among other billion-dollar giants, to create a brand name for a new global product.

I've created or design-directed many famous logo designs and corporate identity programs. The American Express "blue square" design is one of the most recognized trademarks in the world. Other notable marks include those for FMC (Food Machinery Corporation), Heublein, AMI (American Medical International), and Humana.* While these were challenging creative projects, nothing seems to top the exhilaration of naming a sexy-looking sports car, an exotic women's fragrance, a high-tech pocket-size camera, a new wave spirit, or any other consumer product that's on the cutting edge.

When you're out to find the omnipowerful brand name for a major product, your mind is in overdrive twenty-four hours a day. I keep a pen and pad on my night table. Often in my sleep a name idea will awaken me. I don't hear the word spoken, I see it—often depicted on the product in color. Before it fades from my memory, I get up and write it down.

This brings me to the next secret to naming products. You have to be able to close your eyes and see the word you're considering for the name of a product. If you have a problem

---

*The AMI logo and CI program were developed by the author's firm in 1976. The other logos and CI programs were developed during the author's tenure (March 1971 to October 1974) as vice president and head of design at Lippincott & Margulies, New York.

visualizing the word or find yourself trying to spell it, the target buyers of your company's product may have the same problem too. When consumers feel uneasy about a product's name, they will avoid the product—and that translates into a loss of sales.

Jaguar's Sovereign and Vanden Plas sedan sales have stalled in the U.S. market. Both names are difficult for college-educated, white-collar executives to visualize, according to our research findings on automotive names. Honda's Odyssey minivan failed to crack the U.S. truck market, and one has to ask why the company's executives selected *Odyssey,* which is one of the most difficult words to visualize and spell in the English language. Cadillac discontinued the Cimarron due to lagging sales. Launched in 1982 and named after a river in the Southwest, Cimarron, which sounds like the spice cinnamon, was spelled by the auto maker's dealers as Cimaron, Cimmaron, Cimooron, and Symeron in local newspaper advertisements. Purolator courier delivery service went out of business—another difficult name to visualize. Such names as Au Bon Pain breads, Jhirmack shampoo, Belvedere vodka, Capzasin pain reliever, and Germaine Monteil cosmetics have a distinct disadvantage because consumers are less likely to write a name on their shopping list that they can't spell.

Here's a quick test: In a blind tasting of over 300 domestic and imported beers held a decade ago in Chicago, some 5,000 respondents were asked which beer looked most appetizing and tasted the best. If you said Bud Light, Miller Lite, Coors, or Amstel Light, America's best-selling brews, you'd be wrong. The winner hands down was **Schlitz.** So, why didn't **Schlitz** soar to the top in beer sales before the beer maker was purchased by the Stroh Brewery Company in 1997? Here's one reason: Close your eyes and try to visualize this name. It's difficult, correct? Yet you saw this name printed twice in bold type only seconds ago. What's wrong with the name Schlitz?

The word's visual architecture is completely out of balance. There are four consonants before we come to a vowel, which is then followed by two more consonants. The first four letters *SCHL* have no association with any American English word. Unlike the name Bud, it's visually unfriendly; the eye is bombarded with consonant letters. Notice the optical relief and the improvement in visual architecture when we shorten this name to Litz. Now, close your eyes and you should have no problem visualizing the word *Litz.*

"Select a name that will be easy for your customers to visualize" is my advice to chief executive officers who have decided to adopt a new corporate moniker. To get this point across, there's a simple test I give to the board of directors of a corporation that manufactures mass-marketed products. First, I ask the directors if they're college-educated. Usually, they all answer yes. Next, I ask them if they hold a graduate degree. At least two-thirds will say yes. "Then each person on this board probably has a familiarity with over 20,000 American dictionary words. Now, is there anyone here who can spell the word *connoisseur?"* I ask.

Watching these prominent and highly successful business and professional men and women struggling to spell this word on their note pads, I continue, "If you can't spell *connoisseur,* then millions of people who lack your educational and social background will certainly be intimidated by a new corporate name that features such a sophisticated word." It's interesting to note that I've given this test dozens of times and only one person (a woman) knew how to spell this word. "Keep it simple" is one of the seven proven principles of finding the omnipowerful brand name. I rest my case.

The Importance of Phonetics

When we drive we maintain control of the vehicle by how we use the steering wheel and the gas and brake pedals. In creating a brand name, we have control of the word by using a branch of language called phonetics: speech sounds, their production and combination, and their representation by written symbols.

American English words are excellent to work with in the development of product and corporate names because their phonetic sound almost always mirrors the word's dictionary meaning. In short, the lexicographers of our nation's great lan-

guage have done much of the work for us. Let's run through
some examples to help you grasp the important role that phonetics plays in brand name creation.

Action is conveyed by using fast-pronouncing words. The
brand First Alert relies on two such rapid-fire sounding words
to signal the urgency of having this smoke detection unit in
every home. The word *bite* is also fast to pronounce. Notice
that when we change this verb into the gerund *biting,* our pronunciation slows down with the introduction of a second syllable.

We can also speed up or slow down pronunciation by the
choice of the vowel we select to bridge two syllables or words.
The *i* vowel is fast to pronouce, as in "Meribank." We can back
off on the gas pedal by using the long-sounding *u* vowel. Notice the difference when saying "Merubank."

Likewise, you can make a name sound as if it's coming to
a screeching halt by ending it with one of these consonant letters: *k, p, t, x,* and *z. Smack, zap, fact, nix,* and *glitz* are examples. The Hertz car rental gets our attention because it ends
with phonetic impact. Or you can make a name sound as if it's
coasting to a stop by using a long suffix usually ending in the
letter *e. Intelligence, migraine,* and *fragrance* are examples.
Upjohn's Rogaine brand name featuring a long-sounding second syllable seems most fitting for a hair regrowth treatment.

Lightness or heaviness can be conveyed by the choice of
phonetic sounds we combine. For intance, *PizzaSticks* sounds
like a light snack food to munch on before the meal is served.
By contrast, *PizzaRounds* sounds more substantial, as if we
won't have any room left to enjoy the meal.

Brand names can even sound tame or aggressive depending on which part of speech we use. The verb *achieve* seems
docile when compared to the forceful-sounding noun
achiever.

Matisse and Picasso, the great masters of modern art, used
contrasting tones, colors, and shapes to capture our attention.
Similar contrasting techniques are available to you in crafting
the phonetics of a new product name. The 1983 movie *Flash-
dance* was destined to be a blockbuster on the basis of the title
alone. The genius behind this coined name contrasted a new

sound with the word *dance.* Bristol-Myers Squibb's Comtrex cold remedy contrasts a soft-sounding prefix with a hard-hitting suffix to catch our interest. The Vivitar 35mm camera is another example of a product name that contrasts different syllable sounds to capture attention.

As demonstrated, you can alter and shape a word's speech sounds to create a unique tone for a product's name. You can combine words with different speech sounds to produce a name that captures the consumer's imagination. But while you have freedom to be creative, the end result must be a name that is both easy to pronounce and highly appropriate for the product.

Here's another quick test: How do you pronounce the word *Precis,* the name of Mitsubishi Motor Sales of America's economy-priced car? Don't feel dumb if you don't know. According to an article in *The Wall Street Journal,* even the advertising executives at Mitsubishi weren't sure at first. Frances Oda, manager of advertising, was quoted as saying: "We wanted a name that would make consumers think our car is precise. But, frankly, we had different opinions about the best way to pronounce it."

According to the staff reporter, Mitsubishi's executives debated several options, including PRAY-see, PREE-sus, and PRAY-sus. Finally, management settled on PREE-sus and emphasized to its dealers that they all say Precis the same way. What the article didn't mention is that the name Precis sounds more like a drug to fight the onset of a cyst than a car. One wonders why Mitsubishi's marketing leaders went with Precis when the company's consumer testing showed that target buyers of this product would find the name phonetically confusing. Word of mouth is the most effective form of advertising. An ambiguous name will only keep people from touting the product to their friends and business acquaintances.

Unfamiliar pronunciations can pay off if the product is targeted to a subculture or a select group of target buyers. Grey Poupon mustard and *Elle* magazine, both upscale products, may be difficult for the masses to pronounce, but if your primary audience is looking for sophistication, you can benefit from a name that has mystique.

Accent marks may be needed to help consumers pronounce some names. S. C. Johnson's Drano has a bold flat line above the letter *a* to emphasize that the name is pronounced DRAY-no. Names derived from foreign languages must be evaluated for their intelligibility in the U.S. marketplace. A new hotel chain adopted the French word *compris* as its banner. But the name was changed to Compri because management feared Americans would see the letter *s* and pronounce the name com-PRISS.

Brand name pronunciation problems may disappear over time with the aid of accent marks, but there's no guarantee. Take Kamchatka vodka, produced here in the States since the 1950s. The manufacturer wanted a Russian name, and the inspiration came from the Kamchatka Peninsula in Russian Siberia. But after almost a half century of showing in ads the phonetic symbols for the brand name, few Americans have figured out how to say Kamchatka.

Names that get to the top get there because we know them by heart. They are there in our mouths ready to be passed over our lips and made audible to others.

What Works

Using the right letters or syllables in devising a brand name can make a big difference in how the product is both received and perceived by consumers. Here are examples of what works:

■ *Beginning and ending a brand name with the same letter can make the product sound and look like it's on the cutting edge.* Such names are also easy for consumers to remember because of their distinctive linguistic structure. Consider Nissan's Altima car line, Ortho chemicals, L'Oréal beauty products, Elle women's magazine, and IBM's Aptiva personal computers.

- *Adding a vowel to the end of certain American English words can transform the word into a proprietary trademark.* Consider Lyrica, a name my firm created for a new drug to treat psychotropic conditions, and Humana managed health care products. A brand name that ends in *a* can also make the product sound and look friendly and inviting.

- *A created name that ends in the syllable* va, *which means "to go forward" in Latin-based languages, can have a built-in international appeal.* Consider IBM's Aptiva PC and Polaroid's Captiva instant camera. But be careful in selecting the prefix or stem syllable linked with the *va* suffix. The Chevy Nova means "no go" in Latinate languages.

- *Brand names that start with the letters* ch, *which mirror such familiar words as* church, charity, cheerfulness, *and* children, *can bring to mind thoughts of goodness, joy, and fulfillment.* The brand Cheerios, for example, is America's best-selling cereal brand in the $10-billion cereal category. The name has become a hallmark for wholesome and satisfying breakfast and snack foods. The product's name was Cheery Oats when it was first introduced in the 1940s. The name Cheerios captures the playful and distinctive circular-shaped *O* form of this simple wheat product and represents a masterpiece in brand name lexicography. When my firm was retained by Oxford Development to create a brand name for a chain of senior citizen communities, we coined the name Chambrel to suggest feelings of joyfulness and contentment.

- *A simple way to make a product name more masculine is to end it with the vowel* O. Working with the word *terrain,* I coined the brand name Terrano for Nissan's 4×4 sport-utility line marketed in Europe and Japan. Terrano conveys the macho image of a vehicle built for the rugged earth.

- *The letters* Q *and* J *can imply that the product is special.* With the success of the Infiniti car lines Q45 and J30, these letters will continue to be hot for the next few years. Starting a name with the letter *x,* perhaps best identified with the brand name Xerox, was hot in the 1970s, but now it has run its course.

- *If you want to say sex in a subliminal message, selecting a name that starts with the letters se can be the answer.* Consider Gillette's Sensor razor and Cadillac's Seville car line. Both names have sensual overtones. The brand name Secret for a women's deodorant was a smart marketing move too in that the name speaks to the "hidden mystery" of a woman's sexual allure.

- *Brand names that feature or end with the letters um can impart a sense of tranquillity, resolution, and clarity.* A good example is SmithKline Beecham's Tums antacid product. When Abbott/Ross Labs developed a breakthrough in hypoallergenic infant formulas, it turned to my firm to name this retail product. Since a colicky baby can be a parent's nightmare, the challenge was to find a global brand name that conveyed the idea of both nutrition and peacefulness. Research showed us that pediatricians attribute a colic-like syndrome to an irritation in the alimentary canal caused by the infant's inability to digest certain milk protein molecules. Since the noun *aliment* means food nourishment, we coined the brand name Alimentum.

- *To convey the image of advanced technology, scientific breakthrough, or superior performance, the letter z can be very effective if carefully arranged in the product's brand name.* When Pfizer hired my firm to name its new antidepressant drug, the challenge was to find a brand name that could go head-to-head with Eli Lilly's already well-established and best-selling antidepressant Prozac. The name Zoloft was coined to convey the idea of a drug with superior efficacy. Launched first in Europe and then in North America in 1992, Zoloft has taken a huge bite out of Prozac's worldwide market share, and sales reached $1.3 billion in 1996. Glaxo's Zantac, which eclipsed SmithKline's Tagamet as the world's best-selling antiulcer drug, also features the Z initial letter. And the Nissan 300-Z sports car is another example of the effectiveness that this letter can have in conveying the image of advanced technology.

- *Brand names made up of only one syllable and three or four letters can have a strong impact and are easy to remember.* Consider Red and Joy women's fragrances and Fab and Tide detergents.

▪ *Brand names consisting of multiple syllables and nine or more letters can convey stature and importance by their very scale.* Consider Primerica and Microsoft. This is often the case with family surnames too. Rockefeller and Roosevelt have a prestigious sound compared to one-syllable names like Jones and Clark.

▪ *To convey an important characteristic of the product, coining the name from a known English word that communicates that feature can be both fun and very on-target.* Ilford Photo retained my firm to name its new digital imaging system for minilabs. This client wanted a name that reflected the fun and excitement of creating custom prints with graphics and decorative borders. Working with the word *fantasia,* we came up with Printasia as the brand name. Clairol also called upon my firm to name a new women's hair color. The color came out of an aerosol can and was ready to apply in the form of whipped foam. After targeting the word *whimsical,* we created the brand name Whipsical.

▪ *By bridging a vowel with a consonant or a consonant with a consonant when joining two words or syllables you can coin a brand name.* This is essential to achieving a clear phonetic break between one word or syllable and the other. The Delano firm was hired to create a new corporate and marketing name for Houston-based Medenco, a hospital management company. A key image word was *life* since Medenco's business was the preservation of human life. The challenge was to find a one-syllable word starting with a consonant that would form the perfect phonetic marriage with the word *life.* Ideally, it would convey an image of quality in health care delivery. LifeMark was the winning name. In creating a new, simplified marketing identifier for First Federal Savings & Loan of Northern Virgina, a key image word in the company's former name was *federal*—a reminder to the bank's customers that their deposits up to $100,000 were insured by a federal government agency. In shortening the word to *fed,* the goal for the Delano firm was to find a one-syllable bridge word starting with a consonant that would convey quality banking products and service. The name FedStar was coined. The world's best-selling soft drink has the word *ass* in its name, Coca-Cola Cla*ss*ic, but we don't notice it because the syllable break comes between the two *s* consonant letters.

- *Sometimes the omnipowerful brand name can be found within one or two words denoting the essence of a company's product or service.* It's simply a matter of pruning away the letters and syllables hiding a magnificent rose. A recent example is FedEx. What took fourteen characters (Federal Express) to communicate a worldwide delivery service has been reduced to five and nothing has been lost in the contraction. Let's consider an example using one word. Abbott/Ross Laboratories developed a complex liquid nutritive for hospitalized patients requiring long-term tube feeding and the elderly in nursing homes who are unable to consume solid foods. The benefit of this product to the patient was distilled down to the word *longevity.* Working with Abbott/Ross, I concluded that the word *longevity* didn't sound like a food product. But within this word, I was able to find the omnipowerful brand name. By dropping the first syllable and changing the letter *g* to *j* to clarify the word's pronunciation, we coined Jevity, communicating longevity in a simple and highly distinctive trademark.

- *Reinventing the product's generic name can produce the omnipowerful brand name.* An excellent example is Duracell, coined from battery cell. When Dow introduced a convenient self-locking plastic bag to keep food fresh or safe, it captured the product's essence with the simple Ziploc brand name. Making the brand name sound like the product's generic name makes good marketing sense for companies that don't have big advertising dollars to spend. Such was the case when Astra Pharmaceuticals turned to the Delano firm to name its new gauze-like collagen pad to be used by surgeons to halt internal bleeding. Like Johnson & Johnson's Band-Aid brand, the name Hemopad was coined to make the product easy for operating room personnel to remember.

What Doesn't Work

There are letters, prefixes, suffixes, and words that should be avoided in the creation of brand names. Here are some examples:

- *Using a syllable in a brand name that can be spelled in more than one way.* This will only create confusion for people not acquainted with the product's name. Examples: *Sym* can be misspelled *sim, cim,* or *cym. Dyn* can be misspelled *dine. Dys* can be misspelled *dis. Sys* can be misspelled *sis.* And *by* can be misspelled *bi.* The only way to avoid this confusion is to reveal more of the word that's meant to be communicated in the brand name. For example, most physicians register *dynamic circulation* when they hear or see the brand name Dynacirc. However, if contracted to Dyncirc, the communication and spelling of this word would be uncertain.

- *Ending a name with the letters is unless it's Elvis.* The names of most ailments and diseases end in these letters. Examples: syphilis, gingivitis, halitosis, tonsillitis, arthritis, vaginitis, and encephalitis. As discussed later in this book, the name Allegis was changed back to UAL Corp. because it sounded like a skin disease.

- *A brand name featuring a word that can be pronounced in more than one way.* Take the word *acid.* Some people will think of *acidity* and pronounce the name incorrectly. Eli Lilly did a masterful job in naming its anti-ulcer drug Axid, because it communicates the therapeutic indication without any possible mispronunciation.

- *Names that sound like a curse word.* One of humanity's most ingenious inventions was the coining of vulgar words for venting anger and frustration. Who knows how many murders were prevented over the centuries by having those four- and six-letter words that phonetically stress the letters *k, r,* and *t* to fall back on. Ford's German-made Merkur hit a solid brick wall when it was imported to the States. The hard-sounding Merkur name and those noticeable *k* and *r* letters had a subliminal association with a bad word. An Ohio producer of jams and jellies faced this concern head-on and came up with one of advertising's most memorable slogans: "With a name like Smucker's, it has to be good."

- *Featuring a word that's identified with a discreet personal care product.* NYNEX's telecommunication product EZ Max sounds like a new Maxi Pad line extension.* The word *poise* will bring to mind Poise bladder control pads.

*NYNEX was merged into Bell Atlantic in 1997.

▪ *Names that try to be cute in an attempt to gain the consumer's attention.* Many products were doomed from the start by a silly brand name. Here are classic examples: Cow Chip Cookies, Dog Poo Shampoo, and Old Fred's Fine Sex Olives. Then there were the dual packaged shampoos—one branded Country People and the other City People.

▪ *Overused words and syllables, unless your new product will rank in the top three of its category.* Thousands of U.S. banks carry almost the same marketing name. *First National* appears on the facades of 1,681 of them, another 584 start their titles with *Farmers,* 519 lead off with *First State Bank,* 355 with *People's,* 243 with *Security,* and 420 with *State.* In sport and recreational branded products, 580 begin with *pro,* and in automotive and high-tech products, 1,436 feature *pro* in the product's name.

▪ *Coining a brand name with two awkward-sounding syllables.* Pfizer, the maker of Visine, introduced Ocuhist, a medicinal eyedrop formulation targeted at people who suffer eye irritation caused by allergic reactions. The syllable *ocu* comes from the Latin word *oculus,* which means eye. Hist is short for *histamine,* a chemical released in the body that inflames the eye and nose tissues. Phonetically speaking, it's hard to judge which of these two syllables sounds worse. Visine Allergy Relief would have been the perfect name for this product.

5

The Seven Proven Principles

No matter how you cut it or dice it, a brand name is an advertisement for your company's product or product line in its simplest form.

Now, there's a saying in the advertising industry that goes like this: Great advertising is not made by rules or created by guidelines—it comes from creative people. This maxim is misleading and half truthful. I believe this is a more accurate statement: Great advertising comes from creative people who have the wisdom to use proven principles to guide their creations.

Relying on proven principles is not new to creative people in this century. We know that Leonardo da Vinci didn't paint on any arbitrary rectangular proportion. He adhered religiously to the two-dimensional proportions used by the other great masters of his time. They included the golden rectangle and the golden section. These rectangles produced an internal structure within which the artist aligned his major foreground figures, buildings, trees, or whatever. I should note that these rectangular proportions were called *golden* because they were the most pleasing to the eye.

Proven principles do not deter creativity. Quite the contrary, *they're the springboard to creating a genuine selling idea that transcends the product.* Ask the best minds in the advertising industry what it takes to produce great advertising and they will regale you with stories of how their agency's tried-and-true principles led to the creation of their most successful advertisements. Quite frankly, I would be suspicious of an advertising agency that said it doesn't rely on proven principles to guide the creation of its clients' advertisements. Merely relying on its people to be creative, whatever that means, would scare the hell out of me. The same holds true for naming firms.

This brings me back to the primary reason people in ad agencies and corporate marketing and advertising staffs have difficulties in creating great brand names. They don't know the proven principles for naming products and companies. People can get together in a room all day long brainstorming ideas for a product or company name. But will their name ideas be relevant to the product or the company? Will they possess qualities that can catapult the product or the company itself into the realm of marketing stardom?

I know from experience that great brand names have readily identifiable and wholly predictable characteristics. In fact, one could say that I've spent my entire professional career (spanning almost three decades) as a corporate and brand image specialist studying successful names and the communications and image qualities that have made them become famous trademarks worldwide. The result? I've identified seven basic principles in finding what I have coined the "Omnipowerful Brand Name." There are more, but that's getting into fine-tuning, and my goal here is to keep these rules to seven so that you'll remember them. Extensive name research conducted by my firm has shown that most people have difficulty trying to recall seven brand names in any one major product category like beer, cars, and fragrances. Beyond that point there's a real memory lapse. Take this quick test yourself: There are hundreds of women's fragrances sold in America. Try to name more than seven; I'll give you the first one, CHANEL No. 5, to start you off.

The Omnipowerful Brand Name

The omnipowerful brand name represents the quintessential achievement in brand marketing identity. It meets—and in some cases exceeds—all seven of the criteria that are necessary to make even an above-average or me-too product a marketing superstar. By meeting these criteria, your company's brand name has a good chance of becoming a *free agent*—that is, a name that can be marketed or licensed on an array of consumer products having no resemblance to the original product that launched the brand's identity.

Wouldn't you be proud to see people strolling along New York's Fifth Avenue or Rodeo Drive in Beverly Hills wearing casual attire and toting shopping bags adorned with your company's brand name? Wouldn't you be impressed if you attended a neighborhood party and saw your company's brand name emblazoned on trays, glasses, and other household items? Wouldn't you be amazed to see people waiting in line to enter your company's brand name store? Even if these things never happened, wouldn't it be rewarding just to know that consumers and corporate executives around the world hold your company's brand name in high esteem?

Well, here's the good news: Every company, regardless of its business sector, has the ability to brand its products with the omnipowerful brand name. There's no magic required, no need to get a high five- or six-figure dollar budget approval for name creation. You don't need anything except the commitment and determination to find a name that's based on the proven principles in Figure 1.

Questions to Ask Yourself

Is There a Big Idea?

Nothing is more important to the success of a brand name than a big idea that captures the essence, uniqueness, or spirit of the product. The idea should be clear, single-minded, and relevant to consumers, such as that behind Polaroid's Captiva instant camera.

In the mid-1980s, Polaroid's consumer market research showed a need for a new film format that lent itself to a compact portable camera. The company's engineers spent two more years in concept development, and by the late 1980s the

Figure 1. The seven proven principles.

1 *Capture the product's essence, uniqueness, or spirit (ideally in one word) with a big idea.*

2 *Win the consumer's attention, inspire the imagination.*

3 *Insist on a quality of sound that is highly appropriate to the product's category.*

4 *Keep it simple.*

5 *Make it unforgettable by creating a visual image and sound that are recorded in the consumer's mind forever.*

6 *Stay targeted on the product's correct sexual image profile.*

7 *Make believable what you claim the product is capable of delivering.*

new product program was launched under the code name "Joshua." In 1992, Industria Superstudio in New York City developed a new sleek, compact, single-lens-reflex instant camera system with a built-in picture storage and viewing chamber to complement Polaroid's new instant film.

That same year, Polaroid retained my firm to name its new camera system. There were many technological innovations offered by this product that could have been highlighted in the name, such as software programmed into a microprocessor chip to control the camera's auto-focus, auto-exposure, strobe operation, aperture control, shutter speed, and a new film transport system. The chip contained 100 pre-programmed exposure scenarios.

There was a patented new range-finding system called Wink to determine the correct focal zone using infrared light. The camera's optics consisted of a three-dimensional isochromatic lens and complex, precise imaging mirrors that made framing easy and provided superb edge-to-edge sharpness in every picture. The film was in pocket-size format, featuring Polaroid's most technologically advanced instant film chemistry.

We immediately ruled out cute names like Wink because they would convey the image of a cheap, disposable 35mm camera. Polaroid's new instant camera would have a suggested retail price of $139.00, and the ten-photo-print cartridge would be costly—in the same price range as Polaroid's Spectra High Density film. Was a name like Micro 100 a big idea for this camera? We didn't think so. Alternative-priced single-lens-reflex 35mm cameras also boasted microprocessor chips to provide consumers with high-quality imaging solutions.

The big idea here was obvious. For the first time, photographers could watch their pictures develop in the camera's picture storage and viewing chamber, which automatically held up to ten developed and developing photographs. Because pictures were not ejected from the camera after the photo image had been taken, as they were in other Polaroid consumer cameras, the photographer's hands were free for continuous instant picture taking.

The challenge was to find a real or created word that expressed this big idea. Since the camera had a unique built-in film transport system that automatically moved the photo image taken to the storage and viewing chamber in the back of the camera, the names Pivot, Whirlwind, and Instar were ranked among our five best names. But our top name, Captiva, really targeted the essence of the product. It expressed both the pictures "held captive" in the camera's storage chamber and the "captivating photo images" that this product delivered. The name Captiva had all the other qualities of the omnipowerful brand name; it was imaginative, simple, unforgettable, believable, had the right sexual image profile (appealing to both men and women photography enthusiasts), and was clear phonetically—in this case, highly appropriate for an instant photo imaging system.

Two years after Polaroid introduced the Captiva camera in 1993, IBM launched the Aptiva PC computer. I was surprised that Polaroid didn't challenge IBM's Aptiva brand name on the grounds that it diluted the distinctiveness of its Captiva trademark (which, in my opinion, it did). After all, microprocessors are a selling feature of both products and instant imaging products can be made with the IBM Aptiva.

Is It Fresh?

Sometimes the right marketing strategy calls for a name that captures the spirit of the product by avoiding the obvious. For instance, when you're naming a me-too product, you have to cope with the fact that its "essence" and "uniqueness" have probably already been expressed in the names of established competing products. Finding another noun to convey the same message will only produce another me-too name, a name that lacks a genuine selling idea in the minds of consumers.

When I named Nissan's Pathfinder in 1982 and GMC's Yukon in 1989, Pathfinder and Yukon were names that truly captured the essence of a 4×4 sport-utility vehicle built for unpaved road exploration, mountain terrain, and the outback lands. Today, the four-wheeler market has exploded with new products owing to the enormous popularity of these versatile all-weather family vehicles that have essentially wiped away the station wagon. By 1997, sales of these vehicles were already up almost 13 percent from the previous year, and some fifty new model lines are currently in development. The brand monikers selected for these vehicles, such as the Ford Explorer and Expedition, the Mercury Mountaineer, the Lincoln Navigator, the Honda Passport, and the Subaru Forester, all imitate the selling idea behind the Pathfinder and Yukon names. Do American consumers really need another vehicle name implying that it's the "pathfinder" in the sport-utility category? My advice to auto makers is to look at product names that stress lifestyle rather than off-road transportation if they want their new sport-utility vehicle to stand out from the herd.

Then you have situations in which the product's "uniqueness" is not an exciting story to capture in a brand name. Toothpaste certainly comes to mind. Most consumers are unaware that the top-selling toothpaste brands like Crest, Colgate, Aquafresh, and Close-up all contain the same basic ingredients: fluoride, polishing powder, mint or spearmint oil, and seaweed gel, which binds these ingredients together. Yes, line extensions have small amounts of some active ingredient to position the product as providing tartar control, a gum hygiene agent, or a teeth whitener. The advertising mystique that clouds the simple chemistry of these above-average and me-too products has greatly enriched the pockets of Procter & Gamble, Colgate-Palmolive, and others in this billion-dollar industry. Faced with these facts, it makes sense that a brand name for a new toothpaste should speak to the personal benefits of using the product on a daily basis.

Is It Provocative?

No matter what direction a product's name takes, it must win the consumer's attention and stir the imagination. The name of a new product will fall flat on its face if it doesn't arouse interest in the product. The same holds true for the creation of a new business venture or merger name. When Sperry joined forces with Burroughs, the advertised announcement hailed the merger as "The Power of 2." However, the new corporate name, Unisys, received little applause from Wall Street, the nation's business media, and the advertising community. The new organization was quickly dubbed Unisisy. Many felt that either the name Sperry or Burroughs would have served the new merged company far better than a weak-sounding name like Unisys.

Is It Pronounceable?

Having a brand name with unclear phonetics is a sure way to keep the product or product line it endorses from building image power. If consumers can't pronounce your product's brand name, your product will be passed over; it's that simple. You might as well use a Russian word like *Kamchatka* that will steal attention from the product's advertising campaign, theme line, graphics, and packaging design. But clear phonetics do not mean you've hit a home run yet. The sound of the name must be perceived by consumers as being highly appropriate for the product's category.

Is It Simple?

Simplicity is the thread that runs through all great brand names. Mars candy bars, Quaker Oats cereal, Burger King restaurants, Planter's peanuts, Jockey underwear, Ray Ban sunglasses, Honda's Accord, Compaq computers, Citibank retail banking, and Four Seasons hotels, among others, are words and terms that all of us can readily understand and remember. Of course, if you select an eight-syllable word for the name of your product, consumers will inevitably truncate the name for you. Why struggle to pronounce Stolichnaya when you can ask for a "Stoli" on the rocks? Chevy and Olds have become popular shorthand for these two GM division nameplates. Sport car enthusiasts say Vette for Corvette and T-Bird for the vintage two-seater convertible Thunderbird.

Many big-city restaurants have taken gewürztraminer wines off their wine lists because this spicy specialty of Alsace (where it occupies some 20 percent of the vineyards) never moves. "Why?" you ask. This complex five-syllable wine name is too difficult to deal with for most restaurant patrons.

Now, you'd think that the producers and importers of gewürz-traminer wines would pick up on this observation and simplify the name for the American market to make it more order-friendly. If they don't, more California chardonnays will be ordered at restaurant establishments.

When marketing executives hire my firm to name an important product at fees ranging from $50,000 to $150,000, they're naturally expecting us to invent some exotic-sounding brand name that goes beyond their internal naming ability. Yet creating a name that looks and sounds simple takes talent and naming skill. It's like watching Michael Jordan sink a three-pointer with the flick of his wrist. It looks simple—until we try it.

"Keep it simple" also applies to existing product and company names that can be shortened without losing communication value. Take the California-based Great Western Bank; it could be simplified to Great West. The word *bank* is as unnecessary as the words *gas station* following Mobil. And doesn't Great West convey the same thought as Great Western? Earlier I noted that FedEx was a smart name change for Federal Express. But simplifying American Express to AmEx would be a big mistake for this global financial and travel services giant because the prestige of the name gets lost in the truncation.

Is It Believable?

Before you approve any name, ask yourself: Does it over-promise? Does the selling idea behind the name sound a false note? Even when the name for a new product is totally truthful, consumers may find it hard to swallow. Being believable is better than overpromising, especially when consumers have doubts about your company's ability to make a competitive, state-of-the-art product. I've faced this very situation with clients many times, but nothing tops the Ford Motor naming project given to my firm in the fall of 1982.

By the early 1980s, Ford's North American car sales had plummeted to an all-time low. This historic and proud automaker, which pioneered the mass production of affordable, quality-built automotive family transportation, watched its market share fall from 23.6 percent in 1975 to around 16.6 percent in 1981. The once-sought-after Ford LTD and matching Mercury Marquis sedan and wagon lines had lost their luster with American consumers. Their boxy sheet-metal bodies and boring interiors were no match for the new "Euro-looking" cars offered by German and Japanese car makers. To put it mildly, Ford's ass had been kicked enough and it was time to break from tradition and move to the "European approach" in car styling, handling, and performance. Ford's management gave the company's design and engineering chiefs a mandate to come up with new LTD and Marquis models that would blow away the import competition. In short, Ford mounted an all-out counterattack to regain its market share in the upper-middle car segment. In doing so, management was betting the ranch on the sales success of its new car lines, which would make their debut in 1986.

Traditionally, Ford's top sales executives had the last say on the car's styling. Now, those decisions would be left to Ford's design center.

I met with Ken Smith, the marketing strategy chief at Ford's North American Automotive Operations headquarters in Dearborn, Michigan, on October 6, 1992. He insisted on a face-to-face meeting before approving our contract. (The following reflects my recollection of the dialogue that took place between Smith and myself.)

"Well," he said, "I like what I hear, you're hired. Now, let's talk about your brand identity project."

"Before we start the briefing session," I said, "would you sign my copy of the contract I sent you?" I handed it to him.

"Before I sign," remarked Smith, "I need to know what car you drive."

"A 1982 BMW 7331," I answered, wondering if owning an import car had just cost my firm a major new account.

"That's a good car. I drive a foreign car, too," remarked Smith as he signed the contract and handed it back to me.

He went on to talk about the importance of selecting the best name for Ford's new sedans and wagons. "Let me be candid," he said. "If Ford is not successful with these new cars, Ford will no longer be in the automotive business. It's that simple." I didn't know it then, but that remark would become etched in my mind every day that I worked on this project. "Now, let me show you what these new vehicles will look like," Smith said. He reached behind his chair and removed two large mounted color photo prints from a black portfolio case.

If I had held any predetermined doubts that Ford could muster the talent to shed its traditional approach to car styling, I became an instant believer in Fordism the moment my eyes caught sight of these new cars. "Wow!" I exclaimed.

"There are two camps within Ford," said Smith. "One is determined to see the LTD badge carried forward on these new Ford cars because the name is well fixed in the minds of consumers. The second wants a European-inspired name—such as Autobahn—to signal to consumers that Ford's new cars will be as good as or better than competitive-priced European rivals. I need your firm to tell us what is the best direction to take. You don't have to give me your answer today."

"I can tell you now," I said. "The thinking of both camps is wrong. These new car models are revolutionary in design. The LTD name is like placing an old, tired sofa in a newly decorated living room. These cars deserve a fresh and original name and not a reminder of the past mistakes that Ford has made.

"A European-inspired name like Autobahn is not believable," I continued. "Yes, it could be believable if we were naming a new BMW or Mercedes-Benz car, but it's too great a leap for Ford to make at this point in time. It will sound a false note.

"Ford cars are American-built, not European-built. The name should sound American and reflect the broad changes in design, engineering, and production that are under way at the Ford Motor Company. These are my thoughts."

Smith agreed with my thinking. "I want your firm to develop American-sounding names. But I also need a name recommendation that's European-inspired."

"What about the code name Taurus? Is it legally available?" I asked.

"Yes, but management has ruled out the name Taurus for these new cars," answered Smith.

"Taurus happens to be an excellent name for these new cars," I remarked. "The bull conveys strength, power, and endurance. It's distinctive and memorable. Taurus sounds like a well-built American car with mass market appeal. Yes, it's aggressive, but it doesn't overpromise on what the product is capable of delivering."

"Do you really think it's that good a name?" he asked.

"Absolutely!" I exclaimed. "It should be added to the finalist names for these new cars."

I could stop here because we all know that these cars were in fact branded Taurus. But there are valuable lessons in product naming to be learned from the whole story.

Over a six-week period, we considered and evaluated hundreds of real words. We finally arrived at some seventy-five candidates. Words having more than seven letters or three syllables were taken off the list. Our goal was to find the best three or four words that captured this new era in Ford's automotive product history. Destiny, which looked to the future, and Genesis, meaning "to be born" or "the beginning," were selected as finalists. Another finalist name was Legend. Taurus, the name of a constellation between Aries and Orion, of the second sign of the zodiac, and of a mountain range in Asia Minor, was now back in the running.

On another front, we had made good progress in developing a number of coined names. Innotek, inspired by the words *innovation* and *technology,* focused on engineering and design breakthroughs and implied a departure from traditional thinking. Integra, created from the words *integrity* and *integrate,* conveyed products with strong character. I personally felt that one of our best name creations was Lumina. Inspired by the word *luminary,* it focused on the attractiveness of the cars and the clarity of thought that characterized the product's design and technology. Gemma, which in Latin means "a jewel, an object of wealth," stressed high-quality products. These names and several others were chosen as finalists.

Our search for an international word denoting beauty, sophistication, and international style focused primarily on the names of European cities, famous landmarks, and ports of call. Lucerne (Switzerland) was selected as a finalist name. It met the stated image criteria, and the Swiss were known worldwide for product craftsmanship and engineering.

It was November 16, 1982, and I was back again at Ford's North American Automotive Operations headquarters presenting our finalist names to Ken Smith and six or seven other Ford executives. Like a trial attorney making his closing arguments to the jury, I found myself observing the facial expressions, eye contact, and body language of the jurors as I spoke about the communications and image qualities of each finalist. In my closing remarks, I told the panel that all the names passed legal availability and foreign language evaluations. Our thirteen name recommendations for the 1986 Ford and Mercury cars—each displayed graphically and in color on 20 × 30-inch glossy presentation boards—were now in the jury's hands, so to speak. Again, while not verbatim, here's the verbal exchange that followed as based on my recollection and my handwritten notes.

"I think Destiny is an outstanding name. It's friendly, easy to remember, and it sounds like affordable cars," said one executive. Everyone agreed with his assessment.

"The name Innotek gets my vote. It says technology, performance, aerodynamic styling, and quality," said another.

"I don't like the word *no* in the name," remarked an executive.

"Yes, it's true, some people will see this negative, but we believe most people will see the word *innovation*," I countered.

"I agree with Delano's assessment," said a marketing executive.

"Gemma is a good name for the Mercury cars," noted another executive. "I also favor the name Genesis for the Ford cars."

"No way can we go with the name Genesis," stated Smith.

"Why not?" asked an executive who obviously liked the name, too.

"America's Bible Belt is a big market for Ford, and naming

a commercial product after the first book of the Bible might offend Christians," answered Smith.

"I think most Americans understand that the word *genesis* means 'the beginning, the origin of something,' it's not a hallowed word," I remarked. Smith's rigid facial expression told me that he was not about to propose this name to Ford's chairman.

"Is the Delano firm serious about the name Lumina?" questioned another executive in a chuckling tone of voice. "It sounds like a light fixture, not a car name." His remark set off a round of laughter.

"Ford dealers will think we've lost our minds if we called these new cars Lumina," stated another executive.

"Your reactions to this created name come as no surprise," I said. "Lumina is ahead of its time by four or five years. But keep in mind, that's when these new cars will roll off the assembly lines. Trust me, a decade from now people will point to Lumina as one of this century's best automotive names."

"That'll be the day!" snickered an executive.

I learned weeks later that Ford's name committee had selected five of our name recommendations (including Taurus) for a quantitative market study. Lumina, Integra, Legend, and Genesis were ruled out of the running.

A year later, Honda Motor's Acura division announced the names Legend and Integra for its new car model lines. About the same time, AT&T introduced Genesis, a consumer telecommunications product that proved to be an enormous success in the Bible Belt region. Then GM's Chevrolet division launched the Lumina car line in 1989. Chevy's Lumina has ranked among the ten best-selling cars in America since its introduction, and in 1997 more Luminas were sold than any other GM car line. I believe few in the automotive industry will argue today that the Lumina brand name hasn't paid off big time for GM. The creation and management of the Lumina brand will go down in history as one of GM's most brilliant marketing accomplishments. (See Figure 2.)

Now, here's the kicker. In 1990, Ford's North American Automotive Operations marketing group again hired my firm to name a new vehicle line. When I asked Ford's marketing

Figure 2. The 1998 Chevy Lumina.

executives what type of name they were looking for, they replied: "Give us a name like Lumina."

Here are some concrete examples from the marketplace of how the omnipowerful brand name has catapulted the product to global marketing stardom:

- *Nissan's Pathfinder.* The name sells an idea that transcends the product. It's believable because the vehicle is built for off-road exploration. It captures our imagination. The phonetics are clear and the word is easy to visualize. The name is correctly targeted to both men and women buyers of 4×4 sport-utility vehicles.

- *Sony's Walkman.* This simple, uncomplicated name immediately captures both the product's essence and our attention in seven letters. The phonetics are clear and it's believable. The name of the Sony Walkman personal stereo perfectly expresses a product that's built for outdoor recreational activities. Hands down, it's one of the great brand names of this century.

▪ *Planet Hollywood.* This brilliant marketing name rises above the name of any motion picture superstar past or present. It projects the image of an exciting dining experience inspired by the worlds of film and television. It conveys a place where you might rub elbows with the company's four principals (Arnold Schwarzenegger, Bruce Willis, Sylvester Stallone, and Demi Moore) and many more of Hollywood's biggest stars. Whether the stars are there or not, Planet Hollywood houses some of the most memorable film and television memorabilia in the world. The name enjoys excellent phonetics and it's easy to visualize. In just a few years, Planet Hollywood has become a crown jewel in America's number one industry—entertainment.

▪ *Ford's Taurus.* This name (the astrological sign of the bull) conveys power, durability, and reliability. It's believable and it speaks to excellent value for the selling price. At a time when Detroit's car image was in the pits, the Taurus overtook the Honda Accord in 1992 to become America's best-selling car, and it's held that position for five years running.

▪ *Intel's Pentium.* The name captures both the uniqueness of the product and our attention. It's believable and it sounds like the world's leading computer processor. It has an appeal to both male and female buyers and users of personal computers. Whether by design or luck, this created word is a masterpiece in the art of brand lexicography. What gives it architectural symmetry and strength is that the letter *t* is framed on both sides by three letters of approximately the same visual width. Phonetically speaking, the three syllables flow together like a marriage made in heaven.

▪ *Trump.* Perhaps by good fortune or a plan of the gods, the founder's last name happens to convey the spirit of the Trump Organization better than any other word in the American English language. The word *trump,* according to *Webster's,* means "to surpass, outdo; a rank higher than any other, any advantage held in reserve until needed." And when a "trump" can take any card of any other suit, can one find a more appropriate brand name for the owner and operator of big-league casinos than Trump? This one-syllable name is easy to pronounce and visualize, and it's highly distinctive. Best of all, there's a sense of entertainment and magic to the Trump brand name that seems priceless.

- *Absolut Vodka.* This uncomplicated name with a distinctive spelling captures both the essence of the "ultimate" clear vodka and our attention. It enjoys clear phonetics—a quality of sound that's highly appropriate to the spirits category while simultaneously conveying a Scandinavian product. In short, it's the quintessential dream for vodka enthusiasts. It was a smart marketing move to select a name that attracts men and women drinkers of clear spirits. Had this premium, imported vodka been dubbed Brute—a name targeted to men only—it would not, in my judgment, have rocketed to become the number-one import vodka in the country.

- *Calvin Klein's Obsession.* The name captures the uniqueness and spirit of this scent. It's highly imaginative and believable for the product's category. The people at Calvin Klein are astute marketers, and their decision to stick with brand names that are asexual in image for CK's other fragrances, CK1, Eternity, and Escape, has paid off handsomely.

- *Procter & Gamble's Ivory.* Since 1879, this simple brand name has stated the product line's uniqueness (clean-smelling and white) in a five-letter word. This name is correctly positioned to appeal to all family members. When Harvey Procter was searching for a brand name for his then newly invented white, floating, double-bar soap, a reading of Psalm 45 at a Sunday church service inspired the choice of Ivory.

- *Volkswagen's Beetle.* Few brand names in this century have summed up in one word the product's unique statement more effectively than this one. Attention-getting and believable, it has left a lasting visual image of the product in the minds of tens of millions of consumers worldwide. This name correctly positions the product to both men and women. Volkswagen subsequently reintroduced the Beetle nameplate under the name New Beetle for an all-new 1998 car model line. The new car boasts a more luxurious and ergonomically styled interior and superior road-handling performance over the retired Beetle.

The 1974 Beetle (Figure 3) was the last production of the Beetle after thirty years and 11,916,519 cars built at the Volkswagen plant in Wolfsburg, Germany. While aerodynamic in design styling, the New Beetle (Figure 4) retains the look of the original Beetle designed by Dr. Ferdinand Porsche in 1935.

The Misery Name

This is the phonetically imperfect or inappropriate image name selected by a company for the branding of an above-average or excellent product that becomes a marketing drag to live with. I've targeted known retail products past and present (including the trimming of recent dead wood) to demonstrate how the misery name can hold back an exceptional product from ranking number one in its category or even contribute in a significant way to the product's demise in the American marketplace.

Present examples include:

Figure 3. The 1974 Volkswagen Beetle.

Courtesy of Volkswagen of America, Inc.

Figure 4. The "New Beetle" introduced by Volkswagen in 1998.

Courtesy of Volkswagen of America, Inc.

- *Acura.* This brand name was inspired by the word *accurate,* and dropping the second *c* from the name was a big marketing blunder. Even today, some people still pronounce this name "aah-COOR-ah" rather than "AK-u-rah," as in *accurate.* Unclear and awkward brand-name phonetics have kept this exceptional vehicle line from achieving the sales success and market share it deserves.

- *Hyundai's Accent.* The name Accent completely misses the essence of this entry-level car priced under $8,000. Instead, it focuses on trivia. This is a case in which the name greatly understates what the product is capable of delivering for the sticker price. Further, the name is hackneyed, stale, and stodgy. You have a double check mark in the misery column when the Hyundai umbrella brand name is thrown into the picture. Can you think of a more difficult word (Hyundai) for American consumers to spell and pronounce?

- *Chrysler's LHS.* The alphabet-soup brand name LHS says nothing about the essence, uniqueness, or spirit of Chrysler's breathtaking 1998 four-door sedan for the upscale buyer—

and that's a big-time marketing blunder. But there's a valuable lesson here for any marketer who's thinking about naming his product with initials. Among all the letters in the English alphabet, the eighth letter, *H,* is the least desirable for an alphatype consumer brand name. Unless, of course, the product you're naming is a weapon of mass destruction like the H-bomb. "Phonetically a rough breathing aspirate" is how *Webster's* defines the English *h* sound. Take the word *ouch;* it ends with the letter *h* to give this exclamation that "sudden pain" image association. The architecture of Chrysler's LHS name is not pleasing to the eye because the letters *L, H,* and *S* lack any sense of visual compatibility.

▪ *Ketel One Vodka.* We're told by American bartenders and liquor store salespeople that this Dutch vodka handmade from a 300-year-old recipe is the world's best, smoother than Absolut, because three separate and complete distillations take the bite out of the clear spirit. The first one hundred gallons, and the last, are separated and discarded as being either too harsh or too weak. Then only the heart of each distilled batch is rested for six weeks in underground tile-lined tanks where the temperature is carefully monitored. When it emerges, a member of the Nolet family, which has produced this vodka for ten generations, in the old port city of Schiedam, Holland, tastes it to ensure that it has achieved perfection in clarity, conformity, and taste.

So, with such high-quality standards like these and the claim of being the world's perfect vodka, why hasn't Ketel One surpassed Absolut in the premium-priced imported vodka category? Part of the answer can be found in the name Ketel One. It's confusing; the word *One* in the name implies a one-step distilling process, not three separate and complete distillations. The name lacks the ring of a premium-priced product. The Dutch word *ketel* (which means "kettle" in English) is about as appealing and romantic as the word *charcoal.* If you're going to focus on the pot that cooks the juice, then you've got to find a more imaginative word than kettle. Finally, how is the consumer to know that the term *Ketel One* means the top level? To appreciate how ambiguous this name is, imagine seeing a packaged wheat bread branded Oven One or a cough remedy called Test Tube One.

Why Carel Nolet, Sr., the present owner of The Nolet Distillery, didn't brand his company's exported vodka Nolet Vodka baffles the mind from a marketing standpoint. The family name Nolet embraces 300 years of family tradition and it harks back to a time in the seventeenth and eighteenth centuries when Holland became an important center of commerce for the grain trade. After all, it was the availability of Russian grain to Holland that inspired Joannes Nolet in 1691 to be one of the first to open a distillery along the river Maas. And the Nolet distillery remains the most prominent one in Holland today.

Interestingly, the Nolet distillery offers a challenge on its Web site (www.ketelone.com). It invites vodka enthusiasts to taste its Ketel One against the best-selling premium imported vodkas. Nolet suggests pouring an ounce of each vodka at room temperature into separate sniffing glasses. I personally took the challenge and, sure enough, I found Ketel One to be smoother than Stolichnaya and Absolut. Here's a challenge I would like to give to the Nolet family. Using the same bottle design as Ketel One, replace the name Ketel One with Nolet Vodka in the same typeface to keep the test equal graphically. Now compare the two bottles side by side and then ask these two questions: "Which brand name conveys a premium import vodka that deserves to bear the double eagle from the Russian Tsar's own family crest? Which brand name denotes a family tradition that has been handed down from father to son for three centuries?" In the marketing of high-priced spirits, personalized names like Seagram, Remy Martin, and Glenfiddich can have a mystique that transcends the product.

Past examples include:

- *Wang.* This is a classic example of the misery name. Wang sounds like a slang word for something that's hidden behind a man's underpants rather than advanced computer products. It's unfortunate that the company's founder, a legend in the computer field, couldn't put aside his ego to insist on a better marketing name.

- *Sterling.* This British-built family sedan line priced in the $25,000 range moved out of the American market almost as fast as it moved in. The name simply isn't believable for what these products were capable of delivering. Sterling is a good name for an entry-level Rolls-Royce touring sedan.

- *Yugo.* It promised to be a smash hit in the American market in the 1980s with its under $5,000 sticker price. However, Americans laughed at the thought of owning a Yugoslav-made car that sounded like a child's toy—a yo-yo. The Yugos made a quick U-turn back to shores of the Adriatic. This import vehicle would have had a better chance of succeeding in the states if the brand name had captured the real essence of the product (it offered inexpensive local transportation) with an American word like Honda's *Civic.* Highlighting a country that had no credibility for automotive product excellence was a marketing gaffe.

- *Dodge's Dynasty.* Selected to convey the splendor, luxury, spaciousness, and prestige associated with owning an Asian palace, this brand name promised far too much for a modest, economy-priced, lackluster family sedan that was competing with such best-selling vehicles as the Honda Accord. It's also a name that's difficult for most people to visualize. This Dodge model line was discontinued due to lagging sales, and the name Dynasty was mothballed.

- *Apple's Lisa.* Widely known within the inner circle of Apple Computer, Lisa was named after co-founder Steven Jobs's girlfriend at the time. This office PC was the forerunner of the MAC. Priced at $10,000, the Lisa sounded more like a Radio Shack bargain-priced entry-level home computer. This name, targeted as a feminine image product, proved to be a turnoff to many potential male buyers and an insult to female computer operators. Apple retained my firm to evaluate the Lisa name. Warnings not to use Lisa were not heeded by Jobs. Six months after Lisa was launched, it was discontinued.

Here are some current examples of trimming the deadwood:

- *Ford's Aspire and Probe.* Ford announced in early 1998 that it's discontinuing the Aspire and Probe car lines. With Ford's market research muscle, it's hard to imagine that research data could have persuaded management to name a car—or any consumer product for that matter—Aspire. While it means a yearning for something, this word's awkward visual architecture (I'm referring to the first three letters *ASP*) and its phonetic resemblance to the word *expire* should have killed off this name long before it went into market testing. When the prime target buyers of an affordably priced entry-level car are predominantly women in their twenties, why in God's name would you want to name it Probe (implying an unwanted search or penetration) when there are more inviting names for this buying audience?

- *Chrysler's Eagle Talon.* Chrysler finally dumped its decade-old Eagle car brand in 1998. With a U.S. market share of 0.2 percent, Eagle Talons won't be missed by Chrysler dealers. But what may have helped to stall sales is Chrysler's selection of the name Eagle Talon. Imagine if Detroit followed this brand-naming strategy; we'd have the Taurus Horn, the Cougar Paw, the Bronco Hoof, the Mustang Tail, the Aurora Daybreak, and the Mountaineer Hiker. Some automakers just don't seem to get it when it comes to naming cars and trucks. Why? I can only surmise that they don't have a proven naming process in place or an understanding of the principles that could guide them in the development of a great brand name.

What's the lesson here? When you have an above-average-to-excellent product that has the potential for being the number-one best-seller in its category, don't settle for anything less than the omnipowerful brand name.

6

A Proven Process

Getting Started

The first step in the brand name creation process is to identify what are the most compelling aspects of your new product from the buyer's or user's standpoint. These aspects will concern the product's essence, the product's uniqueness, or the product's spirit. Next, use this information to frame the product's "strategic image positioning" in a brief, concise statement. Looking at how Ford positions two different vehicles on its Web site (www.ford.com) will give you a better idea. First, the Contour:

> Ford's 1997 Contour is for people who are ready to step up to responsibility without turning their backs on F-U-N! So much fun, as a matter of fact, you won't believe that Contour really is a 4-door.
>
> This is a lean and agile machine, fun to drive, with room for everyone to enjoy the ride. With its "safety cell" construction and great engines, Contour may be the one thing in your life you don't have to worry about.

Contour's Image Positioning

1. The sum and substance of the Ford Contour: "Wow" and "4-door."

2. The product's uniqueness: A lean and agile machine that's safe and fun to drive.

3. The product's spirit: Youthful, energetic, fun.

Next, the Expedition:

> Ford's 1997 Expedition is the "truck to beat all trucks." It's the full-size 4-wheel drive sport-utility that's as big as the great outdoors. No matter where you travel, the new Ford Expedition gets you there with these go-anywhere features: Best-In-Class Towing; Best-In-Class Passenger Room (seats up to nine); and Comprehensive Safety Features (vehicle includes standard dual air bags).

Expedition's Image Positioning

1. The sum and substance of the Ford Expedition: "Big" and "awesome."

2. The product's uniqueness: The only full-size sport-utility that can seat up to nine; tows up to 8,000 pounds.

3. The product's spirit: Enjoy the great outdoors.

Avenues for Brand Name Exploration

Now you need to target avenues for brand name exploration using the defined strategic image positioning statement, the product's research data, and the consumer's psychological motivation for buying or using the product. There are four steps:

1. Highlight all the words (nouns and adjectives) that describe the product's essence, uniqueness, or spirit in the product's positioning statement. If you can't find at least eight words glaring out at you, it's back to the drawing board.

2. Rate each of the words identified as highly important, important, or not that important. This should narrow the

words down to four or five after the words deemed "not that important" are deleted. Now you've defined the product's "key image profile words." Each of these words represents an avenue for creative brand name exploration.

3. Read over the product's research data with a specific focus on those words (nouns and adjectives) used by test respondents to express their opinions of the product. Highlight all words that convey a positive statement. Now compare these words with the key image profile words selected from the product's positioning statement. The goal here is to identify key image words that may have been overlooked. Words that are rated highly important or important to the product's attributes or spirit represent new key image words and more avenues for brand name exploration.

4. Finally, define in one-line sentences the consumer's psychological motivation for buying or using the product. Highlight all the motivational words (examples: *younger, beautiful, successful, healthier*). Those words selected as highly important and important represent new key image words and additional avenues for name creation.

Defining the Do's and Don'ts

Defining the do's and don'ts serves as a check to ensure that the avenues targeted for brand name creation are on the right track. It also helps to determine the functional name criteria that will guide the creative naming process.

Depending on where the product is in the developmental pipeline, the do's and don'ts can be either general in description or very specific. When Ilford Photo hired my firm to create the brand name for its new digital image system, the system's products were in the manufacturing phase. Because product changes were unlikely at this point, the do's and don'ts were very specific. Here are the criteria we established to guide our creative name development work, and these can serve as a model for framing the naming criteria for almost any product:

The Do's

- *The* ideal *name would convey or enhance the notions of:* creativity, imagination, innovation, excitement, fun, versatility, simplicity, and affordability.

- *The* ideal *name would be:* targeted to the end user (the minilab customer); memorable, distinctive, and attention-getting; easy to pronounce; family-oriented, with appeal to all age groups; friendly and inviting.

- *The* ideal *name would work as an umbrella brand for these products:* reprints of photos without negatives; print restoration; print enlargements and enhancements; print creations; gifts and more; and print with text for special occasions.

- *The* ideal *name would (from an image positioning standpoint):* capture the essence of the system in a unique and memorable fashion, and have no literal (or slang) negative connotations in Spanish, French, Italian, German, Japanese, or English.

The Don'ts

- *The* wrong *name for the system would be:* a total abstraction, offering no clue to the end user as to the attributes of the system; focused only on one product in the system; aimed at the expensive high-end photo lab business— sounding very technical and complex, requiring highly skilled technicians to operate, and difficult to execute graphically.

- *Words that should* not *be featured in the system's name include:* art (sounds too complex); design (suggests that a specialized skill is required); and graphics (a confusing term not understood by many people).

It's also a good idea to identify the words that could be featured in the new product's name. In the case of Ilford's project, we told the client that the following words were deemed relevant to its new digital imaging system and the end products produced, and that the words in boldface would be given the utmost consideration: **create**, creative, creativity; imagination, **image,** amazement, wonder, enjoyment; photo, **print,** outputs; craft, novelty, special occasions; easy, simple; fun, excitement; digital, imaging, system; opportunity (from the customer's viewpoint); versatile, flexible, and creation center.

The winning name we created was Printasia—inspired by the words *print* and *fantasia*. Now, you be the judge and decide whether this name meets the criteria we established at the outset of the naming project.

In developing a new corporate name, the criteria guiding the creative naming process take a different direction. The following criteria established for a major HMO insurance and financial concern can be used as a model in defining the naming criteria for almost any business:

The Do's

- *The* ideal *name would convey or enhance the notions of:* financial strength, solid, and well established; national, a wide geographical reach; customer-driven, service-oriented; high-quality, high-value products; a flexible management style; responsive, caring, friendly professional investment advisers; and a strong niche player.

- *The* ideal *name would be:* focused on mid-size employers and their employees; very memorable; distinctive, attention-getting; easy to pronounce, and easy to spell for college-educated people.

- *The* ideal *name would work as an umbrella brand name for a range of products including managed health care and other traditional insurance products.*

- *The* ideal *name (from an image positioning standpoint) would sound like a company that is:* easy to do business with; professional, very solid; sophisticated, very savvy about its business, and on the move.

The Don'ts

- *The* wrong *name for the new organization would be:* a total abstraction, offering no clue to the attributes of the new company; focused only on managed care; and difficult to execute graphically.

Here's my advice to an executive who has direct responsibility for the naming of a new product, service, or business venture: Get the top executive in your company—the person who will ultimately sign off on the name—to articulate what he believes the name *should* and *should not* do. A company's CEO, president, or marketing chief who says, "I'll know the right name when I see it," or, worse yet, "Find a name that turns me on," should ring a loud alarm bell in your head that your chances of succeeding on such a naming project are slim, if not nonexistent. When I hear statements like these from company CEOs or marketing leaders, I remind them that we're not in the business of picking out ties for our clients because we'd probably pick the ones they wouldn't like. Our mission, I point out, is to find the omnipowerful brand name—a name that will catapult this company's new product or business venture to global marketing stardom. Most top executives respect such directness and realize that they must share their thoughts and insights on what they believe is the *ideal* name.

Defining the Target Buyers and the Competition

It sounds so simple: Target the potential prime buyers or users of your company's new product. The fact is, it's one of the most difficult tasks that can be given to a marketing staff. If you position your company's new product via its brand name, slogan, graphics, package design, and ad theme line to the wrong audience, you may find your new product stuck in deep mud.

This can easily happen if you fail to take into consideration the established audience and perceived image of your company's umbrella brand identity. For example, extensive market research or focus group sessions may indicate that your new product appeals to men and women in their mid-twenties. However, if the traditional buyers and users of your company's other brand-name products are in their fifties and sixties, that needs to be factored into the new product's target-buyer equation. If not, you may discover, after your new product hits the marketplace, that people in their mid-twenties are reluctant to purchase a product when the company's umbrella brand name is associated with a mature audience.

Second- and third-generation products also require careful attention when it comes to defining the product's prime target audience. You can't assume that a redesigned or reformulated next-generation product is going to appeal to the same target audience that the mothballed product did. For example, an automaker's introduction of an entry-level model line may be targeted to first-time car buyers. The second-generation product will more than likely offer a more sophisticated package, advanced design styling and engineering, and safety enhancements. With such improvements, the sticker price will naturally climb upward and the prime target-buyer audience for this vehicle will have moved up in age too. And the first-generation product's name may have to be changed to reflect an all-new product profile.

When the selling environment of a product changes, the target-buyer audience is likely to change, too. Prescription drugs that receive FDA approval to be marketed as over-the-counter (otc) medicines are a good example. SmithKline Beecham's Tagamet 75 otc product, which contains the same antiulcer compound found in prescription Tagamet, is clearly positioned via its colorful and upbeat package design to attract a much younger audience than its Rx counterpart, which is packaged in a standard pharmacy plastic container.

Is there a lesson here? Yes, it's that you can't rely solely on market research to define your product's prime target buyers. What your gut tells you may be more accurate than a three-inch-thick fact-finding research report.

Next, it's essential to know the competition's brands and to make a professional analysis of how they are positioned in the marketplace. This information will help you to:

- Avoid developing a product name that infringes on a competitor's brand.

- Position your product in a way that makes it stand out from the herd.
- Develop a brand strategy that's aimed at niche markets your competitors have not tapped.
- Identify the competitive brands your marketing team has to do battle with in order to win a top-tier ranking.

The Internet is one of the best vehicles through which to obtain this information—assuming your competitors have a Web site. The section on the Internet in Chapter 9 addresses this very subject.

The bottom line is this: You've got to know your product's target-buyer audience and the competition you're up against in order to have the insight that's needed to develop the omni-powerful brand name.

The Sexual Profile

Every brand name has one of five sexual profiles: Total Feminine, A-feminine, A-sexual, A-masculine, and Total Masculine. A-feminine is midway between the A-sexual and Total Feminine image profiles, and likewise for A-masculine on the masculine spectrum. A-feminine means the brand's name leans to the feminine side, but not to the point where the brand is obviously directed to women, as in the Total Feminine name.

The ideal sexual image profile for any brand name usually corresponds to the product's target buyers or users or the product's image positioning. This does not necessarily mean that a product that appeals more to women than to men should have a feminine-sounding brand name. In such situations, an A-sexual brand name may be the wiser choice for the product so as not to turn off male buyers.

For example, a large percentage of men over forty today color their hair to look more youthful, fresh, and energized. The major players in hair color products have all targeted this vast and growing market and have responded by introducing such products as Just for Men. However, because these products are limited in the color and shade ranges offered and are perceived to be not as high-quality as women's hair color products, most men are actually using the latter. Now, which of these three Clairol brands is least likely to turn off the male buyer: Nice 'n Easy, Ultress, or Ms. Clairol? Nice 'n Easy, of course, since it comes closest to being an A-sexual name. Here are some basic guidelines:

- Use a brand name that speaks to the "Total Feminine" or "Total Masculine" image only when the opposite sex is not a measurable factor in the product's strategic marketing plan.
- If the ratio of buyers or users is 75 percent men to 25 percent women, the best sexual image profile for the brand name would be A-masculine. And A-feminine if the ratio is reversed.
- If the ratio of buyers or users is equal or in the range of 60 percent men to 40 percent women, or vice versa, the best sexual image profile for the brand name would be A-sexual.
- Here's the exception. If the motivation for both men and women in buying or using the product is its masculine attraction (powerful, rugged), such as a 4×4 sport-utility vehicle, then the brand name's sexual image profile should be A-masculine (Chevy's Blazer, GMC's Yukon, and Mercury's Mountaineer are examples). Conversely, if the product's appeal to both men and women is its feminine characteristics (soft, smooth), such as toilet paper, then the brand name's sexual image profile should be A-feminine (Charmin, Cottonelle, and Angel Soft are examples).

The Best Two Languages for Brand Name Creation

There are two excellent languages to work with in the pursuit of the omnipowerful brand name regardless of the product's country of origin. American English is number one. Almost all its words enjoy a built-in sound and appearance that mirror the thoughts that run through our brains when we hear and see them (examples: love, hate, fat, thin, high, low, beautiful, ugly, sharp, dull, calm, agitated, and so on).

Italian ranks second. First made a literary language by the poet Dante, this Latin-based language offers an array of words ending in vowels, like *amore,* that have built-in phonetic appeal and a hint of romance to them. Substituting Latin-based words or syllables for English can suggest an international stature for the product. Pfizer's Procardia, a best-selling hypertension drug, and Intel's Pentium, the world's most sought-after computer processor, are two examples (see Figure 5).

The Actual Creation of Brand Names

Now that the positioning statement, the do's and don'ts, target buyers, competition, sexual profile, and avenues for brand name exploration have been defined, market research findings have been studied, and the best languages for name creation

Figure 5. Intel's Pentium II processor.

Courtesy of Intel Corporation's Press Relations.

have been reviewed, it's finally time to have some creative fun. Here's what you can do:

- Develop ten to fifteen names that are based on intuitive thinking. Yes, while it's rare, it's possible that the first, second, or third name that flashes through your mind may be the omnipowerful brand name for the product—that is, of course, if the name is legally available, which is more unlikely than likely. Identify those names that are phonetically appropriate to the product's category and list them in a computer file titled "Candidate Names—Round 1."

- Next, develop ten to fifteen names that suggest a "direct" image association with one or more of the key image words (remembering that nouns and adjectives work best as brand names). Select only those words that have phonetic appropriateness to the product's category and enter them on the same list. Keep in mind that the quality of names, not the quantity of names, is what counts in the brand name creative process.

- Now develop ten to fifteen names (with the aid of reference books and research) that have an "indirect" image association with one or more of the key image words. The goal here is to identify words that are not obvious or merely synonyms of the key image profile words. Target only those names that have phonetic qualities appropriate to the product's category and add them to the list.

- Finally, develop ten to fifteen names that speak to the psychological motivation for buying or using the product. Again, identify those words that have phonetic appropriateness to the product's category and add them to the other names.

Having developed some forty to sixty candidate names, it's time to precheck each name to determine if it's identical or almost identical to an existing U.S. registered trademark or too close in spelling and pronunciation to a competitive product name.

Next, forward the names that passed this preliminary review to the company's designated trademark attorney for computer database trademark and trade name searches to confirm their availability for domestic and international marketing. Don't be surprised if these examinations reduce the first group of candidates by more than a half or two-thirds.

Repeat this name creation process over and over again until you have thirty good candidates that passed all these checkpoints. List these names in a file titled "Candidate Names—Round 2." Now, it's on to Image Mapping.

Image Mapping

A Delano Firm invention, Image Mapping is used to determine which candidate names best fit the product. (See Figure 6.) Here's how it works:

- Think of the Image Map as a globe. Top is "North." Bottom is "South." Right is "East." And left is "West."
- The globe is divided into five horizontal zones. Each zone represents a different level of product price range, quality, and image.
- The top zone is the "Premium-Priced, Highest-Quality Image Product." The second is the "Status Label, High-Quality Image Product." The middle zone represents the "Mainstream Buyer" or the "Competitive-Priced, Good-Quality Image Product." The fourth zone is the "Smart-Value, Good-Quality Image Product." The bottom zone is the "Bargain-Value, Standard-Quality Image Product."
- East represents a "Total Masculine Image Product." The center of the globe represents an "A-sexual Image Product." Midway between East and center is the "A-masculine Image Product." West represents a "Total Feminine Image Product." Midway between West and center is the "A-feminine Image Product."
- After much thought and consideration, place an X in the horizontal zone that best targets the buyers or users of the product and the product's defined sexual profile.

Figure 6. The Delano & Young Firm's Image Map.

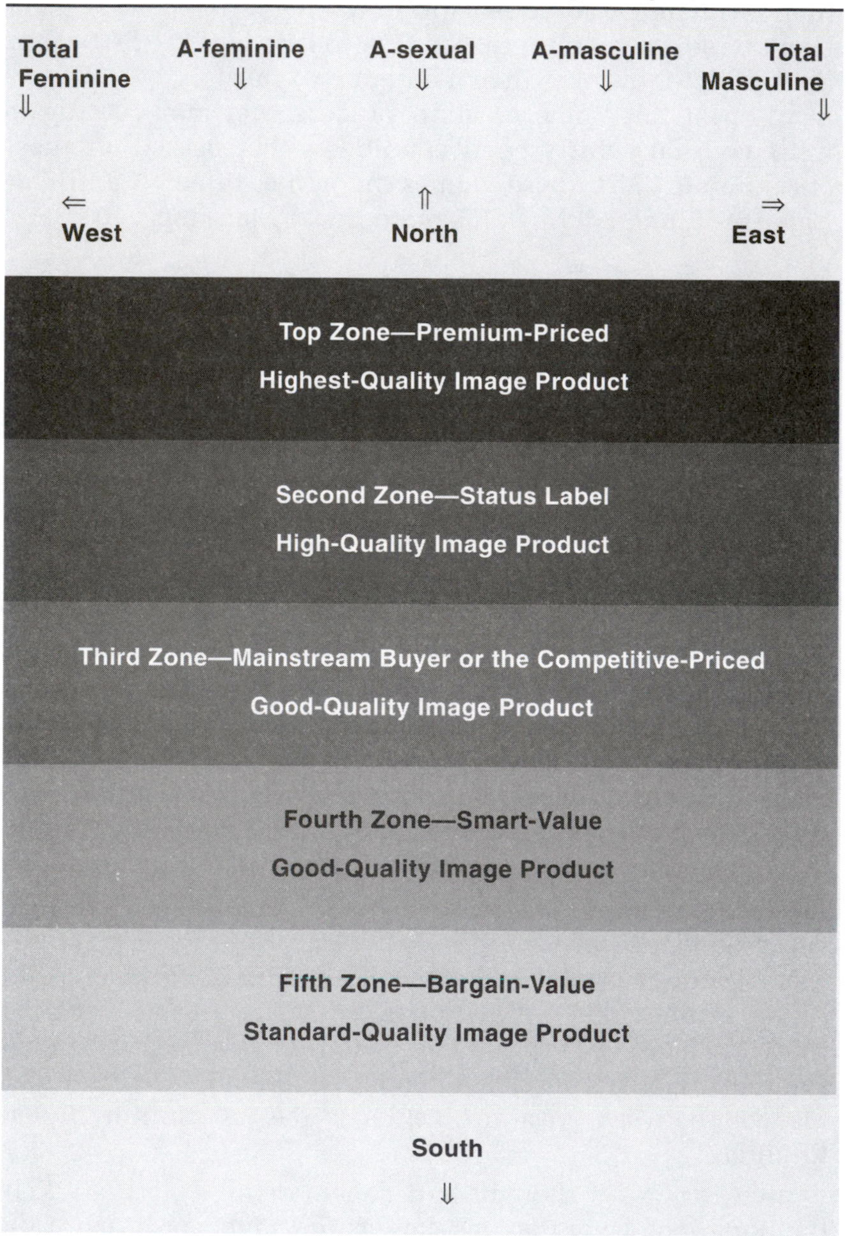

Total Feminine ⇓	A-feminine ⇓	A-sexual ⇓	A-masculine ⇓	Total Masculine ⇓

⇐		⇑		⇒
West		**North**		**East**

Top Zone—Premium-Priced

Highest-Quality Image Product

Second Zone—Status Label

High-Quality Image Product

Third Zone—Mainstream Buyer or the Competitive-Priced

Good-Quality Image Product

Fourth Zone—Smart-Value

Good-Quality Image Product

Fifth Zone—Bargain-Value

Standard-Quality Image Product

South

⇓

• Now refer to the Round 2 candidate names. Enter the first name directly above the X and print out a copy. Repeat this step for all the remaining names on the list.

• After reviewing each candidate, the name team must answer this question: Does the name sound like a product that belongs in this zone and the location within this zone marked X? If the answer is yes, enter the name in a new computer file titled "Candidate Names—Round 3." If the team believes that the name belongs in the target zone but doesn't fit the location marked X, you have two options: You can either alter the name (prefix, stem, suffix, or vowel ending) to correct the sexual profile image problem, or dismiss the name altogether if it cannot be altered without changing the meaning of the name or its positive image association with the product.

If the team concludes that the name belongs in a different zone, basically the same options apply here.

While it's possible through graphics, package design, advertising, and a unique marketing statement to enhance the brand name's perceived image in the minds of consumers, it takes a savvy marketer and the products themselves to pull this off.

Companies willing to risk selecting a brand name that's more than one zone away from the product's correct target image zone should be reminded that many product failures have one thing in common: The brand name selected was well outside the target image zone for the product.

Returning to the Seven Proven Principles

It's time to evaluate the surviving candidate names using the seven proven principles that define the omnipowerful brand name. The goal here is to eliminate any weak or marginal candidate names. Again, your mission is to produce the best five finalist names and five runners-up.

Presenting more than ten names to the company's executive committee means that you or your team haven't worked hard enough in the name development and selection process. President Lincoln said in a letter to a friend: "If I had more time, I would have written a shorter letter." Again, the focus of your efforts should be on the quality of names produced, not the quantity.

Language Reviews

Candidate brand names need to be screened for any literal or slang negative meanings or inappropriate image associations in all major foreign languages, as well as English. A new company or product name can backfire and result in much corporate embarrassment if its literal meaning or image association is negative. Consider these examples from the marketplace:

- The new corporate name Enteron announced in the nation's media was changed to Enron in a matter of days. The board of directors learned that *enteron* is a real word in the English language denoting the last tract of the anal canal. What made this goof-up even more hilarious is that the company's business is in natural gas.

- The new corporate name Allegis (which replaced UAL Corp.) was so hated and attacked by investors, employees, and the nation's press for sounding like a tropical disease or a bad skin rash that within weeks of its debut the board voted to bring back the UAL name after millions had been spent in developing and introducing the Allegis name and a new companywide graphic identity system. The company's chief executive lost his job shortly thereafter. One can only wonder if the name fiasco played a part in his removal.

- The Unisys brand name Unix was quickly dubbed "Eunuchs" by the business media and the public.

- As the story was told to me many years ago by a retired executive, a manager at TWA selected the name *TRANS WORLD AIRLINE TRANSPORT* for the company's air freight business. The name was painted on the company's fleet of transport planes with the initial letter of each word emphasized. To the shock of management, the word *TWAT* appeared. The name was immediately scrapped and the planes repainted.

- I was about to present my firm's number-one name recommendation, *Caprino,* to Seagram's marketing managers for the branding of a new cappuccino-flavored liquor when I was called out of the meeting to take an urgent call from my office. My assistant told me the foreign language evaluations had finally come in on the finalist names for the Seagram's project and that *caprino* means goat dung in Italian.

Testing Your Best Names With Target Buyers

Testing names with target buyers when they haven't been developed by following a proven process is like going out on a blind date: You never know what's going to show up at the door. If the seven principles and proven process offered in this book have been followed, the two names that rank highest in a consumer market test should be the two names your company's name team has identified as the best.

Here's another thought to keep in mind: If you test names that are comparable in intrinsic value to tin, copper, and nickel, one will more than likely come to the top as the winner. At best, the top-ranked name, from a marketing standpoint, will only be worth the value of nickel in the marketplace. In short, *the findings of any name market test are only as good as the quality of names you submit to that test.*

Since 1974, we have gained invaluable knowledge through the testing of countless new product and business names with consumers and other target audiences in North America and in all major markets around the world. One could say that we pioneered the development of name research on a qualitative basis, and our methods of name research on average have proven to be 80 percent projectable as measured by follow-up quantitative name marketing testing performed by our clients' research staffs or independent research companies. Yet, with all the sophisticated tests we've designed over the years, I would still put my money on the findings of a simple name test. I've selected two such tests that should be easy to design and execute for most companies regardless of their size, geographical scope, or industry—and this includes mom-and-pop businesses.

The Simple Name Market Test

We call it the Simple Name Market Test because it's based primarily on spontaneous reaction. Now, here's the kicker: The findings of such an intelligible, inexpensive test (costing under $3,000) have been confirmed eight out of ten times in follow-up, six-figure quantitative market name testing performed for our blue chip clients by independent market research firms.

If this simple qualitative name test is performed correctly and without bias with some thirty target buyers or users of your new product, it will help you to:

- Confirm what names should be ranked first, second, and third.
- Identify names that have an inappropriate image association.
- Spot names with phonetic problems and difficulties in spelling.
- Evaluate each name for its distinctiveness.
- Eliminate individual subjectivity in the name selection process.

Step 1

Explain the new product's essence, uniqueness, or spirit to each of the thirty test respondents in a few short sentences. Reading a three-page description of the product, including technical data, will only overwhelm test respondents and dull their mental ability to react with spontaneity to the names in your test. Test no more than seven names, because most people are unable to recall seven brand names in any product category. If you test twenty names, the findings will only prove that two-thirds of the names could not be recalled and you'll have wasted your time and put a dent into your market research budget without any benefit to your company.

Step 2

Present each name centered on a 15 × 20-inch white board in bold, black Helvetica, or similar *sans serif* typeface. Explain what the *ideal* brand name for the new product should and should not convey (see the section on Defining the Do's and Don'ts). Display the boards in a row and then observe what name or names the test respondent is immediately attracted to without any coaching on your part. Note how the test respondent pronounces each name and any ad lib comments he/she may offer regarding a name's spelling, appearance, or similarity to another known brand name regardless of product category.

When the test respondent is familiarized with all the names, ask which one he/she believes is the best name for the new product followed by second and third choices. If the name he/she first responded to is not among these three names, ask why; you may discover a flaw in a name that was overlooked. After you've conducted these one-on-one sessions, you should have a clear reading on which two or three names are favored by target buyers and users of your new product. If, on the other hand, a majority of the respondents seem to be struggling to identify the top two or three names in the group, it can only mean one of two things: You have done a masterful job in developing an extraordinary group of finalist names, or all the names in the test have serious marketing communication and image weaknesses. Only you can decide what the answer is.

The Numerical-Rating Name Market Test

The second test, which we call the Numerical-Rating Name Market Test, requires rating scores of the finalist and runner-up names given by test respondents and your company's name team. We have found the findings of this inexpensive test to be identical or almost identical with the findings of quantitative market testing (costing in the six figures) of the same names by our clients' independent market research firms.

The total rating score of each finalist name in this test is meant to provide management with a yardstick measurement of the intrinsic value of each name. The scores should be viewed as interpretive assessments of attitudinal responses to the finalist and runner-up names by the new product's target buyers and users.

In any test to determine target buyers' opinions and reactions to brand names for a new product, there's no such thing as an applause meter to register accurately a favorable or unfavorable response. The best way to explain this test is through an example (keep in mind that steps 1 and 2 given above are also part of this test).

In asking consumers if they thought the name Arena was *distinctive* and *memorable* for the brand name of a new minivan, we asked them to rate their opinion on a scale of 5 to 10 points. If the test respondent said 9, we then asked him to qualify that number with a rating of high nine, middle nine, or low nine. When we found that a majority of test respondents answered low nine, we gave the name Arena a score of 9.2 for this criterion, even though other consumers' opinions were less or more favorable.

After conducting numerous internal screening sessions on all the candidate names, our professional evaluation of the *distinctiveness* and *memorability* of the name Arena was 94, using a scale of 50 to 100 points. Averaging together the consumers' score (converting the 9.2 to 92 on the 50 to 100 point scale) and our score, we arrived at a score of 93 for this one criterion.

The same process was used for the other three naming criteria in our test: *phonetics, appropriateness to the product,* and *spontaneous reaction.* When we averaged the scores for each criterion, we arrived at a total score of 94 for this name. The Name Rating Scale we use will help you to appreciate what a total score of 94 means and how you should interpret other scores:

Name Rating Scale

96–100 (Extraordinary). Deserves the utmost consideration.

90–95 (Outstanding). Deserves serious consideration.

80–89 (Above average to very good). A name above 85 deserves thoughtful consideration.

70–79 (Average). Unlikely to catapult a new product into the realm of marketing stardom.

50–69 (Below average to poor). Should be passed over because of its marketing communication and image weaknesses.

In my firm, any name that receives a total score of 79 or lower in this test is eliminated as a finalist or runner-up. Yet we remind our clients not to focus exclusively on those names that scored the highest since any name with a total score of 85 or higher deserves thoughtful consideration as the brand name for the company's new product.

While more time-consuming and costing $5,000 on average, the Numerical-Rating Name Market Test has a distinct advantage over the spontaneous reaction name test. The top executives of most companies usually have a background in finance and numbers are easy for them to understand. A name with a total score of 98 will have more impact on the company's chairman and CEO than your reciting a slew of superlatives to convey the name's marketing communication and image strengths.

Many research people say that they can perform a market test of new product names to determine their image and communication strengths and weaknesses. But how many times do they perform such studies, and what are their techniques? That's a good question to ask your company's research department or any outside research firm. There are many reasons research firms go off track in testing names for a new product, service, or business venture. The following techniques represent five reasons.

1. *Using a focus group session.* While the focus group forum is very useful in testing new product concepts, product packaging, and other issues on which you want to invite debate among test respondents or have them brainstorm ideas, it's not a good forum for name testing. In testing names, you want respondents to openly offer their opinions without being influenced by the comments of others.

2. *Asking test respondents to* associate the names *in the test with a known product category.* Obviously, if a name is unique in its product category, like Arena for the branding of a new vehicle, test respondents will associate this name with sporting products, not cars. Such findings could easily kill what may be a great brand name for the product. The correct question should be: "Is the name Arena *appropriate* for the branding of a new vehicle that boasts a sporty interior and exterior design?"

3. *Presenting each name in the test with a graphic design treatment.* For example, a primary color like red might be used in an attempt to enhance the name's attraction when it could be that it's the choice of color or type design that detracts from the name's intrinsic value.

4. *Digging too deep into the psychological overtones of the name.* When this is carried to an extreme, the findings will blur the name's true marketing communication and image strengths.

5. *Prompting the test respondents to find fault with the names.* The typical question here is: "What else do you find wrong with these names?" When reviewed by management, such comments could easily kill what might well be the omnipowerful brand name for the new product.

Filing "Intent to Use" Trademark Applications

Time is the number-one enemy when you're holding in your hands an unregistered omnipowerful brand name for a major product or business venture. Years ago, we waited until our top names were presented to senior executives and a name was selected by this group before advising our client to file for trademark registration of the approved moniker. Realizing that preparing and scheduling a formal name presentation to top management can take several weeks or even a month or more, we have since put in place a "critical time" strategy designed to minimize our client's risk of losing a great brand name.

A week before we have the findings of the "informal market test" and before the final ranking of the candidate names is made by our project's name team, we have the client's internal or external trademark counsel prepare three "Intent to Use" trademark applications to the U.S. Patent and Trademark Office. The cost per application is $240.00, and checks are drawn and attached to each application.

When the top three names are selected, the attorney completes the applications and the documents are sent by FedEx overnight delivery service to the federal trademark office in Arlington, Virginia. The FedEx receipt provides documentation for the date and time the applications were received by the federal agency, and our client now has an official claim of ownership to our top-ranked brand names. Yes, there's a risk that senior management won't like any of the names selected by our name team. But here's the reasoning behind this "move fast" strategy:

The number of applications filed for U.S. trademarks is expected to soar to a record 30,000 per month on average in the near future. Each business day, some one thousand trademark applications are accepted by the federal trademark office. That means there's a 50 percent chance that another company will file a claim of ownership to the identical or almost identical names of our best candidates within two months' time. If the other company's pending trademark registrations are for goods that are the same or related in some way to our client's new product, there's little or no chance of our best names being granted a U.S. trademark registration if our client files later than that other company. Case in point: We recommended the name Millenium (worth a distinctive spelling) for Oldsmobile's new flagship car, now christened Aurora. The marketing executives were excited about this name, but they wanted to test it first with consumers on the West Coast to

confirm that Millenium was the *ideal* name for the new Oldsmobile sedan. Two weeks later, while the test was in progress,
Mazda filed a trademark application for the name *Millenia* and
that put an end to Millenium.

It still amazes me when some of my clients act as if there's
no need to rush to secure a claim of ownership to a brand
name that's perfect for their product. And there are others who
will hold off for months from filing an application for trademark registration until they've performed a quantitative market survey of our finalist names. Considering how simple and
inexpensive it is to file for an "Intent to Use" trademark, this
is marketing folly at its best.

The Wages of Delay

Some twenty-five years ago, I got my first education on the
importance of taking immediate steps to document a date of
ownership for a trade name or trademark. For a new corporate
moniker, this means reserving the name with the corporate
division in the state or states you plan to do business in and
also applying for federal trademark registration of the name as
a word mark for the company's products and services.

I was vice president and head of graphic design for Lippincott & Margulies, a leading corporate identity consultant
firm with offices in New York. The firm's new client was a
savings and loan based in Jackson, Mississippi. This S&L had
acquired several thrifts throughout Mississippi and it needed
a new unifying visual identity and a statewide marketing umbrella name.

In the early 1970s, the art of naming companies was
emerging as a new specialty offered by a half dozen big-name
corporate identity consultant firms on both coasts. In reality,
these were graphic and packaging design houses that saw the
opportunity to take this creative function away from the advertising agencies at big fees. The profits were also substantial.
Unlike the development of a new corporate logo design, which
was labor-intensive (requiring a large staff of creative and production people), the same $25,000 to $45,000 fee could be
fetched for the creation of a new corporate name. This four-to-

six-week project could easily be handled by one person. Albro Downe, the head of communications planning at L&M, was the naming specialist on this project.

The process used then was simply to develop a master list comprising about one hundred names. The names were listed in two groups: coined words and real words. The list would be reviewed with the client and, with luck, a consensus would be reached on the first, second, and third names. None of the names on the master list was evaluated for legal availability. And little instruction or follow-up guidance was given by the consultant firm to its client about the importance of securing legal ownership of the name it had selected before spending one dollar on design or extending the new moniker to a myriad of media items.

The S&L's president, Tom Scott, and the vice president of marketing, Cleve Brown, favored the name Firstmark. The word *First* was seen as an entity bridge to the organization's historical name: First Federal of Jackson. The name was approved by the bank's board of directors and shareholders. Scott gave L&M the green light to develop a new visual identity system featuring the name Firstmark. The creative fees for a project like this had the potential of reaching into the high six-figure range. This represented a nine-month creative and production effort and entailed the design and architectural drawings for all interior and exterior bank branch signs, including replacement signs for shopping mall roadside pylons.

As the new identity system was being developed, suppliers of one kind or another were coming and going from the offices of L&M and a number of people could easily have seen the name Firstmark. The Firstmark logo design was sent out to reproduction houses for photo enlargements and silk screen colored prints. The approved design was also given to various suppliers for printing and fabrication on a variety of items. All these vendors provided the same services to other New York graphic and corporate identity firms.

During the same time, the S&L's advertising agency based in Jackson had developed new TV commercials and print advertisements to announce the new Firstmark banking name and graphics intrastate. A local public relations firm hired by the S&L devised a plan to attract the attention of statewide media and banking journalists to cover this important name change event. In short, more than a hundred people in New York and Jackson had exposure to the new name and logo design before its public debut.

To the best of my recollection, branch signs were manufactured and ready to be installed; new corporate and branch stationery, business cards, and dozens of customer banking forms were printed, distributed, and ready to be used on the official day of the name change. Everything was in place, and I would guess that the client had about $1 million invested in the bank's new retail marketing identity.

Weeks before the actual name change event, we got the news that the name Firstmark had been filed for financial services in the state of Mississippi by a New York-based financial investment firm. Luth & Katz, the identity consultant working with the investment firm, was a New York competitor of Lippincott & Margulies at that time. What really raised eyebrows, however, was that the other company's Firstmark logo design was almost identical to the one developed by L&M. The color scheme was identical: the word *First* in red, the word *mark* in gray, and the starlike shape above the initial letter *F* also in gray. I attended a meeting held in L&M's New York offices with the client. While not verbatim, I recall an exchange of words that went like this:

"How could this have happened?" asked a very troubled-looking Tom Scott to L&M's co-founder and chairman, Walter Margulies.

"Believe me, Tom, I am more angry than you are over this fiasco," replied Margulies. "I can assure you that every step was taken by my firm to prevent a leak of the name Firstmark and the logo design to outsiders. If someone leaked this, it had to come from your end."

Many questions remained unanswered but the most glaring was this: Why would a New York investment firm reserve the name Firstmark in Mississippi when it had no office or business operation in that state?

Where had the client gone wrong? Scott had instructed his S&L's legal counsel to file the name Firstmark at the state and federal levels but did not stress the urgency of doing this expeditiously. Crucial months passed before legal counsel took action to reserve the bank's new name with the state's banking division, but by then it was too late; Firstmark had been reserved months earlier. There was also an assumption by the client that no competing bank or financial institution in Mississippi would dare to sabotage First Federal of Jackson's new marketing identity. And no one imagined that an out-of-state financial concern would do just that since interstate banking was years away.

Having lost its sizable investment in the Firstmark identity, the bank adopted the name Unifirst. With the financial collapse of many savings and loans in the 1980s, caused by relaxed federal banking regulations, Unifirst numbered among those that failed.

Paying More When You Could Have Paid Less

I have another story on the importance of speed in laying legal claim to a name. Bayer's Acarbose compound falls within the class of alpha glucosidase inhibitors. Prior to the discovery of a glucose inhibitor, drugs to control elevated levels of blood sugar in the body chemically stimulated the pancreas to produce insulin. The downside of these medicines is that they eventually place enormous stress on the pancreas. Acarbose's mode of action takes place in the digestive tract, blocking carbohydrates in the intestines from being absorbed into the blood stream. This drug is directed to tens of millions of people worldwide who have abnormal levels of glucose and are borderline diabetic or diagnosed as having *diabetes mellitus.*

Immediately after the meal, glucose levels peak and then gradually fall into a valley when the meal passes through the digestive tract. Bayer's drug is taken five minutes before the meal to help control these peaks and valleys.

In 1991, the pharmaceutical division of Miles Laboratories (Miles, acquired by Bayer Corp., has since taken the Bayer name) hired my firm to create the brand name for its new Acarbose antidiabetic compound.

The first round of names that we developed focused on

glucose control during the metabolism of carbohydrates in the digestive tract. One of our best names was Metacose. Then we considered names like Panclear to remind physicians that this drug's mode of action stays clear of stimulating the pancreas to produce insulin. Since this drug would be positioned as the first treatment for patients diagnosed as having *diabetes mellitus,* we invented names like Primoda to convey the idea of a "primary mode of action." Although there is no cure for *diabetes mellitus,* this disease is manageable. Therefore, we looked at names like Managest to convey "the management of carbohydrate digestion."

A visit to The New York Public Library on 42nd Street and Fifth Avenue gave me ample reading material on *diabetes mellitus.* I learned that all carbohydrates are digested to monosaccharides and absorbed as such in the form of hexoses, of which glucose is the primary one. Over the next several days I worked on names, attempting to weave in one or two syllables from the word *hexoses.* Looking at Hexobloc, meaning "to block the absorption of hexoses," I laughed out loud at its other interpretive meaning, "to curse the block." Realizing that I was now pursuing naming avenues that were far too complex, I felt it was time to get back to simple concepts.

Reviewing my notes from the new product's briefing session, I had underlined comments made by Miles's new product team such as "before the meal," "before glucose levels rise," and "before other treatment is used to control elevated glucose." Two words stood out: *before* and *glucose.* This led to the name Precose—*pre* meaning "to come before" and *cose,* short for glucose.

Another key word was *meal.* Working with the Latin word *prandium,* which means "meal," and the suffix *dase* from "glucosidase," I came up with the name Prandase.

I called Mel Silver, Miles's trademark counsel, and gave him these two additional names to check out for their availability in the United States and Canada. Silver had already given me the green light on eight of our best names. While I never had the opportunity to meet Silver in person, we seemed to have a meeting of minds when it came down to deciding which names were viable and which might be challenged. His opinions on a brand name's availability were based on sound reasoning and not fear that his approval of a name would come back to haunt him later.

My presentation of our top five finalist names and five runners-up to Miles's pharmaceutical marketing executives went well. They were pleased with our work and agreed that there were three excellent names for the branding of Acarbose. I stressed the importance of making a name decision in the next several days and then having Silver file an application for trademark registration to secure ownership of that name. The Names Report I left with the marketing group stated in capital letters: "FILE TODAY FOR TRADEMARK OWNERSHIP TO THE BEST NAME(S)—DON'T RUN THE RISK OF LOSING ONE OR MORE GREAT NAMES BY FAILING TO TAKE ACTION NOW."

A week later I called the new product director and asked him if a name decision had been made. "I like the name Precose, others like Prandase, and there are a few people who like the third-ranking name in your report," he said.

"Well then," I continued, "you should take ownership of all three names."

"I think a decision will be made in about a month," he added. "We got your message loud and clear that we can lose these names, but people here take their time to make decisions and it will be a year or two before this drug is launched in the U.S. market—so everyone feels there's no rush."

When a month passed, I called the new product leader. He told me that no name decision had been made. Again, I told him that Miles was running the risk of losing our best names. I followed up with a letter to all the members of Miles's new product team repeating this message.

Some six months passed and I took a call from Silver.

"The pharmaceutical division told me to file the name Precose for the Acarbose brand name," he said. "I did a new search on Precose yesterday and discovered that another pharmaceutical company had filed Procose for a drug name three months ago. The pharmaceutical group really wants this name, but Precose is too close to Procose."

"What do you plan to do?" I asked.

"I've already contacted the company that filed Procose. I told the trademark attorney that we're willing to pay them a substantial sum if they'd withdraw the company's trademark application." he answered.

I learned later that a deal was reached, and I suspect that Miles paid the company close to six figures, or double our fee, to develop the name Precose. Of course, it wouldn't have had to pay a premium to own this name had it heeded my counsel. Prandase was taken by Miles Canada as the brand name of Acarbose, and we received a fee to release our intellectual creative rights to this second name. (The fee we charge for a naming project includes the right for our client to take ownership of one name.) Precose is now a globally marketed antidiabetic drug.

When the Client Listens

The next client experience shows that having the rights to the omnipowerful brand name can fetch big bucks even if the name has never appeared on a product or been used in the marketplace.

Greenbelt, Maryland-based Oxford Real Estate Co., is a financial firm owned by Leo Zickler and his managing partners. The company hired my firm to christen a new chain of retirement communities. In April 1986, we advised Oxford to switch its name, too, recommending several alternatives, including Primerica.

When I presented our top finalist names to Oxford's managing partners, the name Primerica inspired a number of wisecracks, like "the prime meat company of America." One partner even remarked, "I hope we didn't pay these guys to come up with this name."

Such remarks are typical whenever you propose a new company name that is not a known word in the English language. I held my ground and told the partners that if they wanted to pass on the name Primerica, they were actually doing my firm a favor because we could easily sell this moniker to a corporate giant at a price three or four times higher than the amount we were receiving from Oxford. I noticed that my remark caught the attention of the company's president, David Lewis, and Zickler, its chairman. They both recognized that this name conveyed a big-league image.

Zickler's investment bankers suggested that he hold off from changing the company's name to Primerica until a major real estate offering by Oxford was completed in six months. We urged him to register the name with the federal trademark office for financial products and services. That advice paid off for Zickler. Not much later, the spoken-for Primerica was recommended by one of our competitors and my old employer Lippincott & Margulies to the American Can Company. Apparently, neither the corporate identity consultant firm nor American Can's management had checked out the availability of this name before getting board approval and announcing to the nation's media that a corporate name change was in the works. Luckily for Oxford, American Can wouldn't be deterred. The bigger firm bought the undisputed rights to the name Primerica for a price close to $300,000. That was more than four times the amount Oxford paid us for this name and the Chambrel signature name that we created for its retirement communities.

There's one thing that should be obvious from these client experiences: Treat all names under consideration as trade secrets. At my firm, all creative naming work is performed in a studio that bears no mention of our firm's name. It's not in an office building where security and maintenance people could have access to the studio in the late evening hours. Brand names for major product introductions are on the list of corporate espionage, and when the stakes are high, competitors have been known to infiltrate a spy as an employee of the building's maintenance or security company. As an added security measure, we meet clients, vendors, and visitors in a different location. When you name products like cars, soft drinks, drugs, fragrances, and computers that will have sales in the billion-dollar range, you can't afford to run the risk of exposing omnipowerful brand names to anyone until you've taken steps to secure a claim of ownership to these names. In the brand naming business, chronic paranoia makes good business sense.

When *Forbes* did a feature story on my firm, the marketing

editor wanted to enhance the piece with a picture of our team at work creating names for a new vehicle. It took us a full day to hand-print hundreds of product names on large sheets, which were tacked up on a wall in our conference room. Here's the kicker: All the names were registered trademarks. Did *Forbes* actually think we'd allow them to show the world our best unregistered brand name creations?

The Presentation of the Finalist Names

The one-minute TV spot opens with scenes of a young John Travolta-looking stud with thick black wavy hair in a black silk shirt, tight black leather pants, and chrome studded boots cruising along the bright lights of Hollywood Boulevard on his low-rider motorcycle. The music playing is "When I meet you tonight," sung by Rod Stewart. The young man spots a gorgeous, shapely young babe with long blonde hair in a low-cut flame-red short dress standing in front of an outdoor bar café. She's surrounded by male admirers. He stops in front of the girl and revs up his bike. She turns and her blue eyes melt into his. In the last scene, she's riding off with the intruder.

Convincing Suzuki

"This is the sexual fantasy that drives the sales of the low-rider motorcycle—also dubbed 'the street bike'—to young men in the 18–25 age bracket," I said to my audience. "Unlike the owners of ten thousand dollar-plus touring bikes equipped to rival most cars in the same price range, the street bike enthusiast likes to explore urban cities and towns alone. He's not a rebel without a cause. More than likely, he's a bank teller or back-room accountant with a college education. But when nighttime comes and he's on his machine cruising the streets, he likes to think of himself as a macho-man who shows up in places where he's not invited."

I had set the stage for the presentation of my firm's top finalist brand name for Suzuki's new low-rider motorcycle made in Japan for the North American market. The Japanese executives, including the president of Suzuki's American operations, were seated along one side of the long conference table. The American marketing, sales, and advertising executives were seated on the opposite side. To create a sense of drama, I decided to use David Letterman's countdown of the top ten. Normally, I would have started with the name that ranked first.

As the names flashed by, one after the other, on the screen in colorful graphics, I noticed that the Japanese executives were taking copious notes on my voice-over comments and the numerical rating score that I gave to each finalist. They were also conversing among themselves in their customary rapid-fire speech. "And now gentlemen," I said, "here's our number-one name recommendation." My finger depressed the projector's forward remote control button and Intruder appeared superimposed over a black and chrome road machine in a bold red logo design outlined in silver.

The faces of the American executives brightened, and to my delight I heard the senior vice president of marketing comment, "That's the name." As I was about to explain the marketing and image rationale for our top finalist, Suzuki's president rose from his chair. All eyes turned to him, including mine. He made the traditional Japanese goodbye gesture of bowing his head slightly and departed from the executive conference room.

"Well, I guess it's back to the drawing board," I whispered to my associate. The remaining Japanese executives immediately began conversing with each other in their native tongue. I glanced across the room at the senior marketing executive hoping to get some signal as to what had just happened. But none was offered.

Just then, the president returned armed with an American dictionary in his right hand. He opened the book and in an excitable voice said, "It says here that 'intruder' means someone who breaks into house . . . why the hell we want to name motorcycle this name?"

"Yes, that's one meaning of the word *intruder,* but it happens to be the right image for this street bike," I replied.

"You agree that this is best name for the U.S. market?" asked the president of the American marketing chief.

"Yes, it is," he answered emphatically.

There was a long pause. "Then we name motorcycle Intruder," declared the president. He walked over to me and smiled. "You make good name." He turned and left the room.

While this ranks as one of the most interesting name presentations I've encountered in my career, I wasn't surprised at the outcome. Having named many import vehicles made by Honda, Nissan, and Subaru, I knew that the Japanese managers respected and almost always heeded the counsel of their American-born senior marketing and salespeople.

The Oldsmobile Story

Now that I think about it, the Oldsmobile name presentation had interesting twists and turns and some rocky moments, too. To appreciate this story, you need to know the background leading up to the presentation.

Throughout the mid-1980s, GM Oldsmobile's management went to sleep at the wheel while its Japanese competitors like Honda were rolling out new cars every two years featuring advanced design styling, ergonomic seating and instrumentation controls, and myriad engineering changes to improve the ride, handling, and power. Ford had introduced the revolutionary-designed Taurus sedans and wagons, which were immensely popular, and Chrysler's designers and engineers were cranking out an array of new cars, trucks, and minivans. Meanwhile, Oldsmobile's product offerings went essentially unchanged for a period of eight years. As a result, the division's unit sales plunged to less than 500,000 by the close of the decade from a level of one million in 1985. Oldsmobile and its dealer network, once the star performers among GM's five car divisions in the 1960s and 1970s, and its oldest car nameplate, were now facing extinction. Rumors abounded in the automobile industry that GM's top management would soon retire the Oldsmobile nameplate and merge its products with those of another division.

To reverse the declining sales nightmare, GM moved Michael Losh, who had proven his talents by revitalizing Pontiac's product lines and the division's morale, over to Oldsmobile in early 1990. When Losh arrived as vice president and general manager of the division, only one new model line (dubbed the N-cars) was being tooled for manufacturing—an entry-level four-door sports sedan and a two-door sports coupe to replace the aging Calais line. Some minor styling changes had been made on the Ciera mid-size car line (tagged the A-Cars), aimed at traditional Oldsmobile buyers, and a prototype design was in development for a new luxury flagship car (code-named the G-car).

Since Losh had inherited the new N- and A-cars, he and his team of engineers, designers, and marketing people went to work to make the G-car a shining example of GM's answer to the Lexus and Mercedes car lines priced in the mid-$30,000 range. Losh was gambling on the G-car to be a smash hit—the vehicle that would turn Oldsmobile's tarnished image around. His only problem was that the G-car would not be rolling off the assembly line until late 1994. This made the success of the N-cars all the more important as a means of convincing Oldsmobile's dealers and GM's managment that better days were ahead for this beleaguered car company.

In February 1990, my firm was hired on the recommendation of Don Parkinson, Oldsmobile's new strategic marketing manager, to name the new A-cars. I had worked with Parkinson in developing brand names for GM Saturn's new cars. Losh, who respected Parkinson's winning drive, his tenacity in challenging his superiors for the advancement of the product, and his intelligence in product design planning, recruited him away from Saturn to join his new Oldsmobile marketing team.

I had kept abreast of Detroit's car and truck sales and the ups and downs of the domestic and foreign auto industry, because naming new vehicles represents about 25 percent of my firm's creative revenues. When I visited Oldsmobile's headquarters in Lansing, Michigan, I was greeted by Parkinson, a stout, rugged-looking man in his early- to mid-forties with a thick crop of blondish-brown hair and matching mustache. I had come prepared to hear about the challenges Oldsmobile faced. What I didn't know was the depth to which the division's morale had sunk—the result of uncertainties about job security among the ranks and of the internal ambushing taking place between the old guard in engineering, design, sales, and manufacturing and the new players on Losh's marketing team. Parkinson understood that we had to know the difficulties we'd be up against and that there would be some people who would do their best to kill any names my firm might recommend even though they might be the best names for the A-cars.

After my discussion with Parkinson, I spent the entire morning in briefing sessions with national and regional sales managers and product planning and market research analysts. In the afternoon, I conducted one-on-one interviews with the heads of engineering, sales, and manufacturing to elicit their thoughts and opinions on the best name for the A-cars. At three o'clock, I visited GM's design center to see full-size prototypes of the vehicles we were naming and to interview the cars' designers. My next interview would be with Losh, who had a satellite office at the design center.

While I was waiting in a small conference room, a man I took to be in his early forties entered holding a large coffee mug. His physical stature and facial features reminded me of the young John Wayne. "Hello," he said, "I'm Michael Losh." His laid-back demeanor, soft-spoken voice, and casual attire masked a bottom-line automotive executive. Quite frankly, his yellow cotton-knit sport shirt and tan slacks were a visual relief to all those dark-gray, double-breasted suits and white French-cuff shirts that I had seen all afternoon. Ten minutes into our discussion about the A-cars, Losh stood up from his chair. "Let me show you the G-car. This is an example of what Oldsmobile's product lines will look like in five years," he said.

The last interview of the day was with the head of market research, Karen Ebben, a tall, large-framed woman in her mid-thirties, who, within three minutes, impressed me as being a woman who, in a historically male industry, had the potential to rise quickly in GM's brand marketing ranks. She was articulate, smart, and saw the big picture. Prepared for our meeting, she quickly spread out on the table a number of charts covering the image positioning of current and future Oldsmobile car product lines.

"The N-cars, our entry-level products, will be called Esteem. Your competitor, Lippincott & Margulies, came up with the name. The tooling has been made to stamp Esteem on the product so this name decision is irrevocable.

"Your firm is naming the A-cars—our value-priced midsize sedans and wagons.

"The next level up is the Oldsmobile Cutlass Supreme; a step above this line is the Oldsmobile 88 Royale, and then the Oldsmobile 98 Regency, the top-of-the-line full luxury sedan," said Ebben.

"Karen," I remarked, "all these names denote the highest-quality product, but not all the products are the same in quality, design, interior appointments, and price range. How on earth is the consumer to know that the Esteem is Oldsmobile's lowest-priced car, the Supreme is mid-priced, and the Royale and Regency are at the high-end sticker price?

"Frank, you're absolutely right, but it's too late to change the name," she answered. "Only Losh could halt manufacturing production at this point."

The next day I broached my concerns about the planned brand-naming strategy for Oldsmobile's complete line of products with Parkinson. He immediately recognized the confusion and told me to bring the subject up with his boss, Michael Grimaldi, Oldsmobile's then general marketing manager. "If you can convince Grimaldi to change the Esteem name, we'll convince Losh, too," he said.

Grimaldi was and is a member of GM's executive fast track. Moving up the GM ladder required the executive to gain hands-on experience in all major facets of the giant automaker's business. Grimaldi was appointed Oldsmobile's marketing chief around the same time that Losh and Parkinson came on board. Having come out of finance, I thought, Grimaldi must possess a keen logical mind. How could I show him through a simple illustration that Oldsmobile's brand-naming strategy had serious marketing flaws?

I met Grimaldi at the Lansing airport gate that evening and

we found a small conference room in which to talk. He looked and carried himself like a rising star at GM. We got down to business and he took out a laminated index card from his attaché case. "Here," he said, handing me the item, "these are the brand characteristics for Oldsmobile's lineup of vehicles."

"Smart, Contemporary Cars That Are Refined, Innovative, Responsive and Balanced" stood out in bold type. "What about the brand names for Oldsmobile's new cars?" I asked.

"They should be distinctive from other car line names," he answered.

This was my opening. "That's the problem," I said. "Oldsmobile's car names lack distinctiveness and individual brand character." I drew four gas station island pumps on a sheet of paper and wrote the name Esteem on the first pump, Supreme on the second, Royale on the third, and Regency on the fourth. I handed him the drawing. "If you saw these four gasoline pumps and wanted to fill your car's tank up with economy-priced fuel, what pump would you select?" I asked.

He grinned and responded, "Esteem is the wrong name. How long will it take your firm to develop a name for the N-cars?"

Within days, our project had expanded to name the new N-cars and the flagship G-car. Our creative naming budget tripled to almost $300,000. The rush was on to develop finalist names for the N-cars within four weeks because the product line was already in production.

The target buyers for the N-cars were 27- to 32-year-olds eager to move up to a more prestigious compact-to-mid-size family car with an international design appearance, quality craftsmanship, technological advances, contemporary interior styling, comfort, and good value for the price. The N-cars offered some of these product attributes and were vastly superior to the Calais line they would replace. However, it was apparent to Parkinson, who inherited the brand management of the N-cars, that GM's designers hadn't pushed the car's design far enough in view of the competition it would face. (As it turned out, the marketplace also agreed with Parkinson's judgment. Oldsmobile's entry-level sports sedan would be totally redesigned for a 1998 introduction, and it would be christened the Alero.)

We went to work developing names that would build a unique brand character for these cars. Almost daily, Parkinson shared with me the insights his group was gleaning about the N-cars' target buyer profile from consumer focus group sessions held at GM's design center. One afternoon he called from his car phone. "We got some good feedback today from consumers. I see our prime market for the N-cars as youthful men and women who are goal setters—career-driven people," he said. "Give it some thought."

"Young achievers," I remarked. Later that evening, Parkinson's words played over and over again in my mind. Then it hit me. The names of Oldsmobile cars praised the product. What about a name that spoke to the buyer's personal ambitions? Parkinson's keen insight led us to develop the finalist name Achiever—one who attains success or a desired end.

We reviewed our finalist names with Grimaldi. "What about changing the spelling of Achiever to Achieva. Wouldn't that make this name more distinctive?" he asked.

"Yes, it would make the name more proprietary," I answered. So, the credit for developing this name not only goes to my firm, but also to Parkinson and Grimaldi.

A second finalist was Focus—conveying the idea of sharpness, clarity, direction, and the ability to zero in on a set goal. A third finalist was Seeker—one who explores, aims at, and pursues a goal with conviction. Agena, a name taken from astronomy, was selected as a fourth finalist because of its interpretive meaning: futuristic, bright, and intelligent. Spontana, our fifth finalist, was inspired by the word *spontaneous*— acting with a natural feeling, on impulse, without any effort.

There were only four days left before our big name presentation to Oldsmobile's management. A quantitative market study of the best names was requested by Grimaldi. An independent research firm, hired by Ebben, performed one-on-one interviews with more than 400 consumers in California's major markets. We had no contact with the research firm, nor would we have any advance knowledge of the research findings until the day of the presentation. Grimaldi wanted us to rank our fi-

Yet, while most of the giants of industry say that they listen to the brand ideas of their people, they don't. Why? Because unless you occupy one of those glamorous corner suites in the corporate tower, your brand ideas are not likely to be taken seriously. What's amusing here—even tragic perhaps—is that the driver who delivers the company's branded products to the retailer or dealer, the secretary who acts as a buffer in addressing customer product complaints, and the trademark lawyer who's privy to the competition's applications for brand registrations, months before these brands enter the marketplace, probably have more insight into what new brands and brand line extensions the company should be developing than the marketing chief who's preoccupied with the company's next sponsored sports event.

If ideas build brands, why is it then that senior executives are unwilling to listen to ideas from their people in middle management, let alone those in associate- and entry-level positions? It comes down to one word: *respect.* Let me expand on what I mean by *respect* here. It's not that management thinks its employees are going to give away proprietary information to the competition or the press; it's that it doesn't feel its people are entitled to know all the facts about the new products that are flowing through the pipelines—or about corporate and brand strategies, contract negotiations with the union, manufacturing problems, and dealer after-sale service performance, among many other sensitive issues. Again, while these organizations say that they treat their people as their most valuable asset, they don't practice what they espouse in their PR releases and annual reports.

As I said earlier, and as Thomas J. Peters and Robert Waterman, Jr., point out in *In Search of Excellence* (Harper & Row, 1982), outstanding brand marketing captains like Ron Bernard, formerly with Abbott/Ross Laboratories, and Don Parkinson, now at GM's Chevrolet Division, roll up their sleeves to get into the action and develop the brand's identity and character alongside their staff members. They don't turn to their assistants and ask them to do it and then stand in judgment of their recommendations. These managers don't operate in a realm of secrecy and deliberately hold back important information from their people.

Building the brand through people also requires senior management to make the work that's performed by all the people involved in the brand's development exciting, fun, and challenging. Again, the lip-service companies do a good job at communicating a sense of excitement and fun in developing the brand. But in reality, they don't give the people responsible for the brand total control, they don't let them stand out, and they don't encourage an entrepreneurial style of brand management.

I take many sales calls from marketing and engineering people who want to know how we can help them to develop the marketing strategy for a new brand. Three minutes into the conversation, it's quite obvious that the person on the other end of the phone knows very little about the brand his company is planning to launch. Yet he starts off by saying that he's been given complete responsibility for the brand's marketing development. "That's wonderful," I think to myself, "we're going to rely on this person for the information we need to build the brand and he's in the dark himself." But something else is also missing: There's no sense of excitement, no zest in his voice for this new brand; it's as if he were ordering an egg white sandwich on white bread without mayonnaise, lettuce, and tomato.

When we're hired by such a company and obliged to work directly with the kind of individual I've just described, here's his pattern. He's late in submitting the materials and information we need to get up to speed; when the information comes in, it's incomplete, with key questions left unanswered. Calls to him are not returned for days and even weeks or more. After the project briefing session, he's no longer accessible to us. He never calls to inquire how the work is progressing or to contribute some new input, such as fact-finding data from on-going consumer market testing of the new product. He doesn't ask for the home telephone numbers of our team members to discuss the project's direction in the evening or over the weekend. In his mind, he's off the hook; his company has retained a leading brand consultancy to devise the brand's strategy and image, and the ball is now in our court. Although he's been invited numerous times to participate with us as a team member, he obviously wants to distance himself from our work and our recommendations. When we present our findings and recommendations to senior management, he doesn't speak up to defend our work because he's afraid to get in the line of fire; he acts as if he doesn't know us, and as if we were hired by another department in the company, and he's merely a spectator.

I have seen a great difference with a number of my firm's big-league clients who have built omnipowerful brands by listening to their people, regardless of their job titles. These senior managers treat their middle-, associate- and entry-level managers as partners, with *respect,* and, perhaps most important of all, as trustworthy colleagues. They call them all by their first names; they share sensitive information with them, and they reward them handsomely for a job well done. In return, these people charged with the responsibility for building the brand are fired up, turned on, and totally committed to the brand's success. They work like people under a "contract to deliver," not like employees working a thirty-five-hour work week.

Staying Consistent With the Brand Name's Image

Don't fret, you're on the right track because that great name you selected has already set the personality, character, and image of the brand. It's simply a matter of staying consistent with—or, better yet, enhancing—that name's personality, character, and image in developing the brand's marketing exposure to consumers. Take Gillette's Good News disposable razors. The simplicity of the product itself, the product's logo and package design, the brand's bright blue color scheme, TV and print advertising all reinforce the image of "good news." By staying consistent with the brand name's image, Gillette's razor brand management made Good News (a great brand name, by the way) a global brand marketing success story for this giant personal care products company.

Now, let's take Ford's Thunderbird. Management's decision to stop production of this classic two-seater sports car, which once rivaled GM's Corvette and became America's dream car in the mid-1950s, remains a real mystery to millions of Americans. The full-size Thunderbird sedan with outdated styling, engineering, and road handling has not followed consumers' perceptions of the brand's untamed image, even though there's no such wild creature on earth called thunderbird. Since the 1970s, the brand's advertising has never presented the product in a compelling and memorable way. While the look of the 1957 T-Bird convertible has left an indelible image in the minds of countless people worldwide, the same cannot be said for the last two decades of T-Birds. Here's a quick test: Can you describe what the 1997 Thunderbird looks like? Can you recall one Thunderbird commercial that has aired on TV over the past ten years? Do you know what the Thunderbird brand logo looks like? If you answered no to these three questions, it should come as no surprise to you that Ford announced in early March 1997 that it was discontinuing production of the Thunderbird due to lagging sales.

Where else did Ford go wrong in managing one of the most famous American brands of this century? It wasn't creative and daring enough with the product and the product's image in a fiercely competitive industry, and these are essential elements in building the omnipowerful brand.

When I think about Ford's massacre of the Thunderbird brand, I recall what the comedian Alan King said: "Coca-Cola had ninety-eight percent of the American cola soft drink market and Pepsi had the other two percent. So what did the marketing chieftains at Coca-Cola do? They changed the product's formula." Automakers build sports cars to build image power for their other best-selling vehicles like sport-utilities, minivans, and pickup trucks.

Ford's way to save face is to introduce a breathtaking two-seater sports car that will rival GM's all-new Corvette C5 (*Motor Trend*'s 1997 car of the year) in aerodynamic styling, engineering, and road performance—and if such a vehicle is in prototype form or being tooled today, it's my professional opinion that this new roadster should have a fresh and imaginative brand name or at least add a modifying word to Thunderbird to denote a new era for this retired brand. When Volkswagen brought back the Beetle in early 1998, it was a smart marketing decision to brand the redesigned car the "New Beetle." Sales have been so brisk (as of May 1998), that there's a six-week wait on the car. Those that have New Beetles are selling them for up to $3,000 more than the car's sticker price. But this may be the exception, not the norm. History has shown that brands that have been mothballed for many years are forever labeled—fairly or unfairly—with either company or product failure. GM Buick resurrected the Roadmaster brand in the 1990s, and the car line was discontinued in 1996 due to lagging sales. Examples of other mothballed car brands include the Hudson, Packard, DeSoto, Studebaker, Avanti, Delorean, Chevy's Vega, Cadillac's LaSalle, Ford's Pinto, and Pontiac's Fiero.

Being Creative and Daring

I have heard many tales of creative brand marketing, but nothing has amused me more than the story told me by Eric Hilton of the Hilton Hotel and Inn empire. It shows that creativity and daring take an entrepreneurial spirit.

It was 1977, and I was interviewing Hilton in his Houston office. To my surprise, he was down-to-earth and unpretentious.

Hilton was a member of Medenco's board and a major stockholder. As I stated earlier, my firm was hired by Medenco to rename the company and to develop a new corporate and brand marketing program. What I didn't tell you was that the company's then chairman, William Mackey, was counting on me to a create an award-winning program that would attract the interest of a bigger fish in the health care industry—in other words, a company willing to pay perhaps three times Medenco's stock price to acquire this fifth-ranking, publicly held hospital chain. A year or two after the company launched the LifeMark name and the new brand marketing program we created, Mackey got his wish: American Medical International (my firm created AMI's corporate identity, too) paid a premium price for LifeMark.

I must confess that I was anxious to hear Hilton's thoughts on building a new brand identity for Medenco. He was the only person on my client's interview list with hands-on marketing experience. This was at a time when for-profit hospital companies were under intense scrutiny by federal and state health care regulators and receiving harsh criticism from community leaders for making profits from the care of sick and dying people.

"I supported Mackey in his decision to hire your firm. The name Medenco sounds like a dental supply company, not a hospital chain," said Hilton. "Mackey and his team know how to work numbers, but they've got a lot to learn about creating a brand image, and that's why you're here."

"What's your view of the hospital business?" I asked.

"It's really no different from the hotel and inn business. You rent rooms and suites out by the hour, day, or week and the big profits come from providing in-house services to the room's occupant," replied Hilton. "The goal is to get the guest to spend his money in your establishment. That's where brand marketing comes into the picture. But it takes inventiveness— let me give you an example:

"Some years back, one of our inns hired a college student during the summer break to run the soda fountain station. A month passed and the executive chef became alarmed when he saw a huge bill for egg deliveries—double the amount of eggs used by the inn's kitchen in any given month. The chef soon discovered that the additional egg orders were requested by the new soda fountain worker. Confronting the young man, he asked, 'You received from the kitchen this month some 1,000 eggs. There are no eggs on the soda fountain menu. What did you do with all these eggs?'

" 'Well,' he answered, 'when people order a milk shake, I ask them if they want a Hilton Shake with one egg or a Hilton Gold Shake with two eggs. Most people go for the Hilton Gold Shake. Don't worry, I add the price for each egg to the customer's bill.' " (Note, I am relying on my recall of this story and I may not be accurate about these product names, but I think you get the point.)

Here's what makes this story special: The soda fountain worker not only created new menu items; he single-handedly built a brand (Hilton Shake) and a brand line extension (Hilton Gold Shake) as an upscale version of the product. Further, he gave customers the option of having one or two eggs in their shakes but didn't offer them a nonegg shake, which would have been less profitable to the Hilton Inn. This young man's entrepreneurial marketing spirit coupled with his devotion to the brand's value to the customer racked up big soda fountain sales that summer for one Hilton Inn.

Many marketers will say it takes big advertising and promotion dollars to build a brand. What they forget is that many brands backed by big advertising dollars have vanished from the marketplace. Almost always, creativity doesn't require one more dollar than what is already being spent on building the brand. If you're a candy manufacturer and your automated production line stamps out 100,000 candy bars today, you need the same number of candy bar wrappers to keep the product protected and fresh. Creativity is changing the copy and graphics you print on these wrappers. Whether you're printing wrappers with the old graphics or new graphics, you still need to print wrappers, so where is the big added expense here? Let's draw on a real-life example to drive this point home.

Bloomingdale's and Its Brown Bags

It was the decade of the 1920s. The United States under the leadership of President Calvin Coolidge and then of Herbert Hoover was focused on building business and creating jobs up until the market crash of 1929. And it was big business for the Prohibition bootlegger. Carmakers were busy cranking out Tin Lizzies. *Show Boat* by Edna Ferber and *The Saga of Billy the Kid* by Walter Noble Burns were best-sellers. And Bloomingdale's introduced small brown paper bags with a printed message on them.

According to Bloomingdale's public relations department, when the first printed bag appeared in 1922, it featured a special fiftieth anniversary message to Bloomie's customers. It was the store's first recognition that the simple brown bag for protecting and carrying purchased items could be used to make a statement about the store itself.

But in the 1920s, the idea of a shopping bag—an expansive paper sack with convenient carrying handles—was still some three decades away. When Bloomingdale's introduced its first shopping bag in 1954, the bag's design featured a rose on one face panel, a gloved hand with an umbrella on the other, and the store's old-fashioned script logo. This design was used throughout the 1950s, and at Christmas time the graphics were replaced with a sprig of evergreen and a candy cane.

"It wasn't until 1961, when Bloomingdale's launched its first storewide import fair, that it commissioned a special shopping bag for the occasion. The French Tarot-card design, which flagrantly omitted the store's name, became the first in a long series of 'designer' bags that raised the medium to a level of fine art. For the next two decades the bags were created by artists, photographers, graphic designers, even fashion designers. Most bags were seasonal. Some came back for repeat performances. Examples of these bags can be seen to this day in museum collections worldwide," said the public relations department.

Then in 1973, the linen department needed a really big bag to hold pillows and blankets. Joan Glynn, then head of advertising for the Bloomingdale's stores, came up with the whimsical idea of the "big brown bag" and naming it as such (in poster-size type) on the bag's two face panels. Within days of its debut on the streets of Manhattan, Bloomingdale's big brown bag made national and international news. The "little brown bag," for cosmetics and accessories, followed a year later. And the "medium brown bag" was added in 1992.

Bloomingdale's "big brown bag" showed the retail giants of the world that building the brand's awareness takes creativity—*not* big advertising bucks. This is *powerbat* marketing at its best. (See Figure 8.)

Around the world today, these distinctive bags are as readily identifiable with the Bloomingdale's franchise as the

Figure 8. Bloomingdale's "big brown bag."

Courtesy of Bloomingdale's Public Relations Dept., New York.

golden arches are with McDonald's. And this one creative idea has done more to reinvigorate the Bloomingdale's brand than any advertising campaign the company has ever launched.

A Proven Process for Packaging the Brand

The Image Mapping process (see Chapter 6) is designed to help you determine which finalist brand name will work best for your new product. This same process will also define the creative direction to take in developing the brand's packaging. The term *packaging* here refers to the way you orchestrate the brand's verbal and visual identity for consumers, not to the physical packaging protecting the product.

Too often, the selection of the brand's logo, color, selling environment, and other media items is based on management's preferences or the subjective thinking of one individual. This is how brands get derailed even before they enter the marketplace. To keep the brand's visual identity on track, there must be an image target to aim at. If you follow the Image Mapping process invented by my firm, you'll find your target in one of five image zones.

Here's a quick review of the Image Map: Top is "North." Bottom is "South." Right is "East." And left is "West." The map is divided into five horizontal zones, each of which represents a different level of product price range, quality, and image.

The top zone is the "Premium-Priced, Highest-Quality Image Product." The second is the "Status Label, High-Quality Image Product." The middle zone represents the "Mainstream Buyer" or the "Competitive-Priced, Good-Quality Image Product." The fourth zone is the "Smart-Value, Good-Quality Image Product." The bottom zone is the "Bargain-Value, Standard-Quality Image Product."

East represents a "Total Masculine Image Product." The center of the map represents an "A-sexual Image Product." Midway between East and center is the "A-masculine Image Product." West represents a "Total Feminine Image Product." Midway between West and center is the "A-feminine Image Product."

Now, place an X in the horizontal zone that best targets the buyers or users of the product and the product's defined sexual profile. I've selected three established retail brands to demonstrate how Image Mapping works in the creation of the brand's visual identity. First up is one of the world's most recognizable and sought-after brands.

The Chanel Label

The brand Chanel, named after Coco Chanel, the company's founder and Paris's famed designer of women's couture fashion, fits in the Image Map's top zone, "Premium-Priced, Highest-Quality Image Product." The Chanel brand also represents a "Total Feminine Image Product." So, the X belongs in the northwestern corner of the Image Map reflecting the brand's affluent buyers—women looking to make a fashion statement with Chanel's designer-label apparel, shoes, bags, jewelry, beautification products, and Coco Chanel-inspired fragrances like CHANEL No. 5 and Coco.

When you have a great brand name like Chanel that's directly on target with the X placed in the top zone of the Image Map, then *less is usually more* in the creation of the brand's packaging—logo design, color, product identity and labeling, and other media items that have direct or indirect influence on the brand's image. And that's precisely the strategy Coco Chanel used—and her predecessors have used—to build the omnipowerful Chanel brand. For example, the Chanel trademark is based on a simple design—two interlocking Cs in a circle. The Chanel brand logo is straightforward—a contemporary sans serif typeface. These brand marks represent a fashion statement that's timeless. In fact, the Chanel trademark has become such a global status symbol that an international black market thrives on selling Chanel look-alike handbags with gold chain straps and bearing those gold interlocking Cs. The brand's colors are gold, black, and white—again, a visual statement that supports the X positioned in the top zone of the Image Map. Whenever I think about the classic design of the Chanel fragrance and cosmetic boxes, it brings back fond memories.

As a youngster, it was always a treat for me to visit the Bloomingdale's store in New Rochelle, New York (Bloomingdale's in the mid-1950s was the crown jewel of department stores in Westchester County. The store closed its doors some years later, and New Rochelle, once a community as quaint and charming as its nearby neighbor Bronxville is today, has never regained its footing). The Chanel fragrance counter on the store's main level was a must stop for my mother. And I must confess, I was absolutely enchanted by those glossy white fragrance boxes with the words "Parfum No. 5 CHANEL Paris" appearing in black on the face panel. Today, amid the maze of department store fragrance counters and the visual clutter of brand-name fragrance boxes featuring leopard spots, flowers, colored stripes, diamonds, pearls, and just about everything else, those same classic white Chanel boxes still stand out from the herd.

Overcoming the Barneys Name

Barneys is a high-end limited chain of department stores (with signature stores in midtown Manhattan's high-rent shopping district and Beverly Hills's famed golden triangle) catering to upscale men and women willing to pay a premium price for a "status label." The stores are known for their avant-garde window displays, glamorous merchandising environments, designer-label clothing lines and accessories, jewelry, and home furnishings. Yet the name Barneys sounds like a carnival character or a discount toy store catering to budget-minded consumers looking for "Bargain-Value, Standard-Quality Image Products." "Barney the Dinosaur" has taken the toy industry by storm and then there's Flintstone's "Barney Rubble." Barneys also conjures up images of a Seventh Avenue men's discount clothing outlet.

Based on Barneys's flagship stores, the X belongs in the center of the second zone of the Image Map—reflecting a "Status Label, High-Quality, A-sexual Image Product." For people unfamiliar with the Barneys brand, the X seems to fit in the southeast corner of the Image Map—reflecting a "Bargain-Value, Masculine Image Product." Many established and new brands have this problem: The reality of the brand is heading north on the Image Map, but the perceived image of the brand's name is heading south of the border.

When there is a wide gap between reality and the perceptions of reality created by the brand's name, the packaging of the brand can help to narrow that gap. In the case of Barneys, it created a department store with an elegant architectural facade and window awnings to complement the store's award-winning interior design. It devised an upscale and contemporary-looking brand logo that is featured on shopping bags, merchandising tags, executive stationery, store credit card, in-store counter cards, print advertisements, and TV commercials, among other media items that impart an image consistent with a brand in the second zone of the Image Map. All these images project an A-sexual image profile since Barneys customers are both men and women.

Brand color also played an important role in positioning

the Barneys brand as a status label. Certainly, a warm red or orange color would only add to the image of a value-priced department store like Kmart. Bringing a tone of formality, sophistication, and style to the Barneys brand, the brand's logo appears in white Roman-style letters on a solid black background, indicative of formal evening attire. But Barneys didn't stop there. A white-gloved doorman greets customers at the front door, a concierge seated behind a reception desk in the entrance foyer provides helpful information to out-of-town visitors, and the gourmet restaurant in its flagship stores rivals any nearby three-star restaurant—all symbols of status and prestige.

The lesson here is that you can elevate perceptions of the brand's name to a higher zone on the Image Map by introducing image-building graphics and advertising and selling environments and by surrounding the brand with upscale images. Again, keep in mind that we usually learn about a brand from friends and business acquaintances, and this means that our first impressions are formed by what our ears hear.

Shifting the Image of Sears

Yes, with the right creative packaging, a well-established brand can shift from A-masculine to A-feminine on the Image Map. Just look at the Sears brand for proof. America's oldest surviving one-stop-shopping department store, Sears has stood for almost every product you'd ever need in your home or away from home, and that includes tires, batteries, and other replacement parts for your car.

The Sears brand has always represented the "Mainstream Buyer" or the "Competitive-Priced, Good-Quality Image Product"—zone three on the Image Map. The brand's sexual image profile was more A-masculine than A-sexual and definitely not A-feminine. Therein lay the image problem. Career-minded, college-educated women did not perceive the Sears brand as a "status label" for women's fashions and beautification products. After all, if you walk past garden tractors, table saws, gallons of house paint, washing and drying machines, and then turn the corner and find racks of dresses, blouses, and suits, it would be hard for any woman, especially today's working woman, to take Sears seriously about being in touch with her fashion and glamor needs.

With respect to the Image Map, Sears had to find a way to move the Sears brand image from A-masculine to A-feminine to add sex appeal to its lines of women's fashions. Yet it could not afford to alienate the male buyers of its men's fashions, appliances, electronics, tools, and lawn and garden, fitness, home improvement, and automotive products. Revamping the entire Sears brand identity to an A-feminine profile would have done just that. The new packaging of the Sears brand for women had to be done through advertising. The ad theme that was born, "Come See the Softer Side of Sears!" is advertising at its very best. The theme says "There are many sides of Sears" to appeal to men, women, and kids, but the "Softer side" is exclusively for women. The people responsible for creating this brilliant brand positioning each deserve to receive a million-dollar check from Sears, Roebuck and Company.

Changing established perceptions of a brand's sexual image within its correct target zone on the Image Map also requires skillful brand orchestration. Like millions of American men, I grew up wearing Jockey brand underwear; it was the macho thing to do. While Fruit of the Loom men's cotton briefs were a "bargain-value" compared to Jockey's higher price tag, for me that word *fruit* was like dangling a cross in the face of Dracula. Then one day I learned that the exclusive men's Jockey brand would appear on women's briefs. While I didn't lose any sleep over this news, my three decades of faithful loyalty to this brand slowly evaporated and I began buying designer-label briefs like Calvin Klein. I guess you could say that Jockey for Her opened the door for me to explore other A-sexual brands targeted to men and women. Had the underwear maker packaged its new women's line under a different brand and introduced a new brand logo, I would have continued to view Jockey as a men's brand.

Some brands that are "Total Masculine" or "Total Feminine" are unable to shift to an A-sexual image position regardless of how they're packaged. Can you envision His Maiden-

Form or His Wonder Bra men's briefs and the brand's name printed across the brief's front elastic band as it is with Calvin Klein underwear?

In packaging the brand, one has to remember that all brand names, even the great ones, have imperfections. However, when the imperfection has to do with the name's pronunciation, it usually cannot be corrected with graphics. People look at the Acura car brand logo in advertisements and still say aah-COOR-ah and not AK-u-rah as it's pronounced on TV commercials. Honda's division could place a stress mark over the letters *AC* in the logo or spell the name phonetically in advertisements to help people learn the intended phonetic sound. But that would flag the fact that management selected a brand name that was imperfect in phonetic quality, and then consumers might wonder if the product line also has imperfections. The irony here is that Honda's management selected the Acura name to convey accuracy.

Repackaging can also pay off in big dividends. In April 1996, Bob Carlisle's newly released CD album titled *Shades of Grace* was aimed at the Christian audience. One of the best songs on the album, "Butterfly Kisses," quickly gained popularity with a universal audience. By the end of April 1997, 150,000 albums had been sold, and that's considered respectable by any record company's yardstick. But the story gets better. When Diadim/Jive took over the marketing of Carlisle's album in May 1997, management wisely repackaged the CD. The album was retitled *Butterfly Kisses, Shades of Grace* and the album's cover was redesigned to depict a striking graphic of a butterfly. Within two months of the repackaging, the recording artist was presented with a double platinum award; translated, that means two million albums had been sold, and sales continue to rack up at a brisk pace as I speak.

Now, for those business executives out there who believe that a great product deserves a great name, I suggest that you enlarge and frame the paragraph above and place it on your desk so that when others suggest a mediocre name for your company's next product, you can point to the *Butterfly Kisses* album success story.

Never Taking On Anything Second-Rate

The "never take on anything second-rate" philosophy has made Ralph Lauren the individual a billionaire and his world-class brands one of the biggest marketing success stories in the rag trade industry. In 1996, the worldwide revenues for both Polo and Ralph Lauren branded products topped $5 billion. Not bad for a fashion designer (named Ralph Lifshitz at birth) who was the youngest of four children and reared in a middle-class Bronx, New York, neighborhood, never graduated from college, and was turned down as a designer for Brooks Brothers men's fashions because his portfolio lacked panache.

Lauren got his first break in 1967, when his collection of tie creations for Beau Brummell Ties quickly made fashion news. Convinced that he had the entrepreneurial drive to start his own tie company, he launched the Polo brand in 1968—and his success with this venture has never slowed down.

Interestingly, men's ties are probably the last thing you think of when you consider the vast array of products that have made the Polo and Ralph Lauren brands household names. And that list keeps growing. In addition to his men's fashion lines and Polo fragrances, which still represent the company's core revenue base, there are Ralph Lauren's sleepwear, bath towels, footwear, underwear, swimwear, hosiery, hats, scarves, leather wallets, handbags, luggage, eyewear, jewelry, timepieces, furniture, and even a new line of wall paint, according to a recent article in *Investor's Business Daily*. He is considered one of America's most astute financiers and a master at licensing the all-powerful Ralph Lauren and Polo brands.

Packaging the brand is Lauren's hallmark. His company's print ads are unmistakably Polo. The photo images of opulence, comfort, and self-confidence all speak to an era of great wealth in American history. But Lauren's genius in brand marketing has also inspired new lines of merchandise that span many countries and cultures, from the English aristocracy to the Eastern prep school look to America's Western frontier and the untamed lands of Africa. So successful are the Lauren brands around the world that the company has recently gone public.

Confounding other American fashion designers, Lauren opened his first Ralph Lauren brand store in 1971. Today, there are over one hundred Polo and Ralph Lauren stores in the United States and overseas, according to the *IBD* article. Add to this his Polo lines and boutiques with specialty stores and upscale department stores like Bloomingdale's and Neiman Marcus, and it's clear why the Lauren brands have become a powerhouse of unparalleled proportion.

But what is it that makes Lauren's Polo and Ralph Lauren brands different from the brands of other fashion design houses? One obvious answer is Lauren's control over his brands and the products that bear his brand names. Like others in the high-end retail business who have built omnipowerful brands, Lauren is a perfectionist. His flagship store in midtown Manhattan was given more than seventeen coats of paint before the doors were opened to the public, as stated in the same article.

Another answer can be found in Lauren's gift for borrowing a fashion idea that's been floating around for centuries and giving it that unique Lauren touch and look that makes it *his* brand-property. "I recreate it to my liking and taste," said Lauren in the December 1996 issue of *Town & Country* magazine. A third answer is that he's taken products that we all use or need to get through the day and night and made them into sought-after fashion package statements. But I believe the fundamental answer lies in Lauren's insistence on only taking on new ventures and product lines that can be branded and marketed in the Polo/Ralph Lauren first-class way.

The Decline and Resurrection of a Status Symbol

Taking on second-rate products has greatly devalued many world-class brands. The best example I can think of in this half-century is GM's Cadillac Motor Car Division. In the 1940s, 1950s, and 1960s, the Cadillac name not only stood for excellence, it was the "gold standard" for all American brands. After all, consider some of Cadillac's engineering and design achievements from 1909, the year GM purchased Cadillac, through the 1950s: In 1912, Cadillac was the first to equip cars with electric starting, lighting, and ignition; in 1915, Cadillac was the first to offer a production car with a V-type, water-cooled, eight-cylinder engine; in 1926, Cadillac was the first to offer a comprehensive service repair policy on a nationwide basis; in 1927, Cadillac introduced the LaSalle, the first car to be completely designed by a "stylist," Harley Earl; in 1928, Cadillac was the first to install security plate glass as standard equipment; in 1937, a Cadillac-built V8 broke all previous stock car records at the Indianapolis Motor Speedway; in 1943, Cadillac was presented with the Army-Navy "E" award for excellence in production of war equipment; in 1944, Cadillac produced the M-24, the fastest and most maneuverable light combat tank; then in 1948, Cadillac changed the look of all automobiles with the introduction of the tail fin; and in 1954, Cadillac was the first to provide power steering as standard equipment on its entire line of cars.

In the fifties and sixties, a common expression heard in executive suites was: "We want to be the Cadillac in our industry." Can any manufacturer or marketer conceive of having a more enviable brand position in the U.S. marketplace? Well, GM Cadillac had it and the automaker lost it by inept brand management. Then in the late 1970s, the redesigned Sevilles were introduced and were quickly labeled one of the ugliest luxury sedans ever offered by an American automaker. Then, in 1982, it rolled out the Cimarron, a boxy-looking compact family sedan that from an engineering and design standpoint didn't deserve to have the Chevrolet badge, let alone the Cadillac crest mounted on the car's hood. To further devalue the brand, the design styling and interior appointments offered in Cadillac's DeVille line in the 1980s were hard to differentiate from less expensive Buick and Oldsmobile competing models built on the same platforms and equipped with the same suspension and power trains. In 1987, with much PR hype, Cadillac introduced the Allante. The Allante became America's first automobile to compete in the European-dominated ultraluxury segment of the market. The two-seat convertible body and interior were designed and built in Italy by Pininfarina, then shipped aboard 747 cargo planes to Detroit for assembly of suspension, power train, and other components.

However, many automotive journalists had little praise for the Allante's exterior and interior styling, engineering, performance, and road handling. Some went so far as to label the two-seater second-rate in view of the car's hefty $50,000 sticker price. Ultimately, the buyers for an ultraluxury European-styled sports car were not convinced that the Allante was a good investment as compared with other European-made two-seater sports cars like the Mercedes SL offered in the same price range. With disappointing unit sales, GM discontinued production of the Allante a few years after its debut—yet another blow to Cadillac's historical reputation as a builder of world-class vehicles.

Sometimes it takes a series of product failures and egg on your face to galvanize a company's management into action. In 1992, with the introduction of the totally redesigned and reengineered Sevilles and Eldorados, Cadillac once again showed the world that it could design and build luxury cars that are indicative of the famous Cadillac crest symbol. In its continued quest to make the Cadillac brand represent a higher standard, the company's engineers developed the first four-valve-per-cylinder V8, the 4.6-liter Northstar. Like previous powerplants from Cadillac, the new V8, introduced in 1993, set new standards for the automotive industry. Constructed with both aluminum block and cylinder heads, the Northstar features sixteen new patents, including a unique "limp home" feature that allows the engine to operate without coolant for more than fifty miles in emergency situations, according to Cadillac's milestones Web site fact sheet. Another first-rate feature of the Northstar powerplant is minimized maintenance in the form of scheduled tune-up intervals being extended to 100,000 miles.

In 1994, Cadillac continued its first-rate product standards of excellence with the totally redesigned DeVille, including the Sedan DeVille and the all-new DeVille Concours, which became the company's premium six-passenger luxury sedan featuring the Northstar system. No longer were automotive journalists referring to Cadillac's lineup of cars as look-alikes to other GM division cars.

Another Cadillac milestone was reached in 1996 with the

debut of its OnStar system. OnStar combines advanced technology and customer service to provide Cadillac car owners and drivers with safety and security, all at the touch of a button. OnStar brings many of the conveniences we have in our homes to the Cadillac vehicle. The system includes an automatic notification of air bag deployment, with an emergency signal being sent to the OnStar Center. The adviser will try to reach the car's driver via the on-board cellular phone. If the driver doesn't answer, the adviser will dispatch help. Push the "emergency" button on the OnStar phone and an OnStar adviser will locate your position by global satellite technology and contact help, and remain on the line until it arrives. If you're locked out, you can call OnStar toll-free and an adviser will send a signal to the car that unlocks it automatically. If your Cadillac security system has been activated, an OnStar adviser will call to verify if the car has been stolen. If it has, then OnStar tracks the vehicle and calls the police. If you're stuck with a flat tire or have run out of gas, an adviser will pinpoint the car's location and dispatch help. And an OnStar adviser can also make hotel and restaurant reservations and help find the nearest cash machine. Now, that's the stuff that builds the omnipowerful brand.

Even with all these new product milestones and innovative services since the start of the 1990s, however, I have yet to hear one of my clients or anyone else say, "We want to be the Cadillac in our industry." Have you? This should send a clear message to all marketers that once brand image power is lost, it can come back but usually not to the same level it once enjoyed. I believe that the management presiding over the Pan Am brand knows well what I'm talking about.

When a Shave Is Not Just a Shave

Many first-rate brands have become second-rate simply because the competition introduced a superior product. Instead of marshaling all its resources to match or beat out the better product, the brand's maker took no action at all. The result? These brands, once household names, have either disappeared from the marketplace or they've lost significant market share, becoming, at best, niche brands catering to a loyal but ever dwindling audience. Let me offer an example from my own experience.

When I was a youngster, Barbasol was the best-known name in brush shaving cream, with a brand heritage that dated back to the 1920s. It also happened to be my father's favorite because he thought it offered a great shave. When I became a teenager, my father switched to Rise aerosol foam shave cream. This innovative shave cream in an aerosol can was more convenient to use, and when you dispensed it on your hand you could actually see those tiny shaving bubbles rise before your very eyes. However, those gas-injected soap bubbles would also deflate before your very eyes if you didn't start shaving right away. When I was in my mid-twenties, my father switched brands again—this time to Gillette's Foamy. When I asked him why he had changed brands, he told me that Foamy stayed thick and moist after it was applied to his face and that he got the best shave ever—it was that simple.

The Barbasol brand line today is marketed by Pfizer Consumer Health Care Division. The product comes in three forms: an 11-ounce aerosol foam shave cream can, a 7-ounce shave gel can, and a brushless shave cream in 7.5-ounce tubes and 9.5-ounce jars. Pfizer has repositioned the once traditional "beard buster" brand as a "terrific value" available in seven thick and rich varieties, including Original, Menthol, Lemon/Lime, Skin Conditioner, Sensitive Skin, Aloe, and Extra Protection. It has also added more emollients for a supersmooth close shave and given the product line's packaging a new, contemporary face-lift. But Barbasol is far from regaining its position as the best-selling shaving brand in America despite these product enhancements and image-building attempts by Pfizer. Why is it that many men pass over Barbasol for another popular brand like Gillette's Foamy when in reality it's on a par with the best-selling shaving creams and gels? I believe the answer can be found in eight letters—Barbasol.

The era of the barber shaving the town's hero as depicted in Hollywood Western movies is history. The term *barber* is also ancient history; call your men's hair stylist a barber today and you'll have insulted his training, skill, and profession.

Shaving creams and gels for men and women are now high-tech products, like the superthin razors that glide smoothly through these lubricants to give a close shave. My advice to Pfizer's Health Care Division is to rename its excellent shaving product with a twenty-first-century brand name. Then don't be surprised if in a few years the product line soars to the category's best-seller.

The Barbasol brand offers another lesson for marketers. Don't brand your product with a name that relates to a job title that may change tomorrow. Secretaries are now called administrative assistants, while commercial artists, as they were called up to the mid-1960s, have taken the title of graphic designers, and stock brokers are now referred to as asset managers, to give a few examples.

The Rise brand is still in the marketplace, but it has lost its foam, so to speak, to more innovative and high-tech shaving creams and gels. Rise happens to be a great brand name for a shaving cream, but the product needs to be reinvented and repositioned as first rate; if not, I predict that the Rise brand will disappear from the marketplace before we see the next century.

You can sell first-rate products and offer first-rate customer service, but if your establishment looks second-rate to consumers, you may not survive in a fiercely competitive industry. A classic example is B. Altman & Company, an upscale department store chain that went out of business in the late 1980s.

Gone: All the Old Familiar Places

When B. Altman opened its department store in White Plains, New York, in the 1930s, it was "the ultimate place to shop" for affluent consumers living in Westchester County, lower Connecticut, and parts of New Jersey. B. Altman's flagship store in Manhattan was already known for its top-of-the-line brands, and its White Plains store quickly gained a reputation for excellent customer service (before and after the sale) and a no-hassle return policy. But what really drew people from miles around to B. Altman in White Plains was a chance to shop in or just browse around one of the most glamorous and modern-istic suburban department stores on the East Coast at that time. The success of B. Altman's White Plains store attracted the attention of other big-name department chains and it wasn't long before Saks Fifth Avenue, Neiman Marcus, and Blooming-dale's erected their department stores within walking distance of B. Altman's store.

When a friend told me that B. Altman was having a going-out-of-business sale, I made a point of visiting the White Plains store in the hope of finding some quality-crafted chairs and sofas made by Baker and John Widdicomb, among other noted furniture houses. Entering on the main level brought back memories of my last visit to this store in the early 1970s. As I looked around, it was obvious that Altman's hadn't kept the store's interior decor up to date and in pristine condition. Display counters and merchandising departments were ex-actly the same as I had remembered they were some two dec-ades earlier; only now they showed visible signs of decay from years of wear and tear. As I toured the store, I noticed painted walls and doors that were marred and dented and patches of floor carpeting that were worn thin enough to reveal the con-crete pavement underneath. The desks used by salespeople to write orders were covered with scratches and the wood veneer was lifting up around the edges. Everything looked old and tired. "How can any department store chain compete with the Neiman Marcuses of this world when it allows one of its flag-ship stores to deteriorate to this condition?" I asked myself. The answer was obvious with the going-out-of-business sale. It can't.

Famous retailer names like Bonwit Teller, Gimbel's, and Abraham & Strauss have since followed in B. Altman's foot-steps. But the recent announcement by the parent of F. W. Woolworth Co. that all Woolworth brand name stores (some 400 in America) were closing their doors took most Americans by complete surprise. For 117 years, the Woolworth store, a fixture on America's urban landscape, was a place in which city dwellers and town folks could find an array of general household items like sewing thread at a fair-value price. In those classic Woolworth stores with a lunch counter or table restaurant service, the liverwurst sandwich on rye bread garnished with a pickle slice and priced under two dollars was the day's main entrée for many senior citizens and office workers living on a tight budget. What brought the demise of Woolworth? Management said that Woolworth stores had been losing money for years, that the chain could no longer compete with the likes of Kmart and Wal-Mart. Some retail analysts were quick to place the blame on management's failure to move Woolworth stores to the suburbs decades ago. I happen to agree with other analysts who said that Woolworth stores were no longer a friendly, fun, and up-to-date place to shop in—it's that simple.

The lesson here is that you can be second-best in your industry and still be a success in the marketplace, but when you become second-rate or take on anything that's second-rate, you're not going to build the omnipowerful brand.

Nothing Like an Innovative Product to Build the Omnipowerful Brand

The theory that "If you build it, they'll come" works here. Nothing beats having a breakthrough product that works as advertised to build the brand's image big time with consumers, investors, employees, and other key company audiences.

The Energizer, Neptune, Ziploc, Coppertone, and Pyrex Brands

For example, Eveready added pounds of muscle to its already popular Energizer brand when the company was the first to introduce an alkaline on-battery tester in May 1996, and remains the only brand in the marketplace to offer the tester on four cell sizes that make up 94 percent of all batteries sold.

Eveready's scientists and product engineers came up with a simple way to test the power of Energizer batteries on the spot and within seconds. When you press two green spots firmly, the word *Good* appears in the tester window at full power. When the tester remains black, less than 25 percent of the power is remaining. The test uses thermochromatic technology that measures the power left in a battery on the basis of the heat generated in the tester.

A convenient on-battery tester and a response rate that is almost three times quicker than the competition's tester has made Energizer alkaline batteries the number one choice for consumers. Mix together this invention with a reputation for making batteries that are long-lasting, dependable, and guaranteed to perform as advertised with a great brand name like Energizer, which captures the product's essence in one captivating word, and amusing advertising (the Energizer pink bunny that keeps going, and going, and going) and you have the recipe for the omnipowerful brand in the alkaline battery category.

Clothes washers are clothes washers, aren't they? After all, they all have an upright basin and an agitator, don't they? No. Not since Maytag's engineers made an unusual discovery. They learned that by turning the standard wash basket on its side and removing the agitator, you have a revolutionary way to clean clothes. Without the agitator taking up space, this high-efficiency washer branded Neptune has the largest capacity of any residential washer on the market.

The new Maytag washer not only looks different; it also uses only half the water and energy of conventional machines, while removing tough stains better. In addition, without the agitator, Neptune's innovative and gentle wash action actually protects your clothes from getting tangled and damaged.

Demand for the new Neptune washer has been so high that Maytag has had to offer a special reservation program to the public. When you have a breakthrough product like this that reflects years of research, innovation, testing, and engineering coupled with residential and commercial products that for more than half a century have represented dependability, you've got real substance behind the brand.

Yet, in my opinion, Maytag's management needs to make improvements in the packaging of the Maytag umbrella brand and product brands like Neptune. The company's logo and graphics and the visual presentation of Maytag's washers, driers, dishwashers, refrigerators, and cooking products to consumers don't reflect the future in high-efficiency residential and commercial products born from innovative engineering. Check out Maytag's Web site (www.maytag.com) and you'll find its line depicted in cartoon-like drawings embellished with trite and corny graphic images.

It's hard to believe that a quarter of a century ago (1972), Dow Brands created a revolutionary product in food storage—the zippered bag—when it introduced Ziploc Brand Bags. Today, Ziploc Brand Bags remain America's favorite. Ziploc freezer bags come in five convenient sizes, vegetable bags are available in the gallon size, storage bags are quart-size for all-purpose use, and then there are Ziploc sandwich and snack-size bags, perfect for small-size food and leftovers.

But always in the pursuit of discovering a better mouse-trap, Dow Brands improved Ziploc Brand Bags with the innovative Colorloc zipper. Locking the bag's yellow and blue zippers together makes a green seal—visual evidence that the bag's zipper is closed tight so that liquids won't seep out and the food inside will stay fresh.

Again, we have a great product brand name like Ziploc and the Colorloc feature trademark, which capture both the product's uniqueness and the consumer's attention, married to a simple but brilliant idea that transforms an everyday household product like a clear plastic storage bag into a miracle reusable package for an array of products that extends far beyond the kitchen. This is the stuff of which omnipowerful brands are built.

It's amazing how something as simple as changing the product's color can make consumers believe that the product is a revolutionary breakthrough. Take sunscreen branded products, which are a billion-dollar industry. There are hundreds of them out there vying for the consumer's attention. Research has shown that people under twenty years of age, especially kids, run the greatest risk of getting badly burned from too much exposure to the sun's rays and that in later life this could result in skin moles turning cancerous. When kids use these off-white cream-based products, it's hard to tell if the sunscreen was applied to all their exposed skin. So, what did the people who make Coppertone branded products do?

They introduced a purple-colored sunscreen for kids that's fun to apply and makes it easy for them to spot areas on their skin not yet protected by the product. After applying the sunscreen, the purple color fades away to a natural skin tone.

Energizer batteries, Ziploc Brand Bags, and Coppertone sunscreen products demonstrate that innovation doesn't mean that you have to reinvent the wheel. Making the product more convenient and easy to use for the consumer is in itself an innovation that builds the brand. Corning's Pyrex Portables is one more example.

Here's a scenario that takes place thousands of times every day in America. You're invited to a friend's party and you tell the host that you'll bake a casserole dish to add to the party's buffet. When the baked casserole comes out of the oven, you've got the problem of keeping it hot and packing it for transport. If you're like most people, you'll wrap it with aluminum foil and place it in a supermarket brown bag and hope that the contents won't spill over and leak through the bag onto your car's back seat while en route to the party. The people at Corning Consumer Products Company came up with a solution to this age-old problem. They developed Pyrex Portables, good-looking, insulated food travel bags that are leak-proof and designed to keep casserole dishes, pies, or whatever hot upon arrival. Pyrex Portables come in different sizes and shapes to accommodate a wide selection of oven-proof cookware marketed under the notable Pyrex brand label. I can't think of a better name to give to this new product line than Portables, can you? Now, that's using the old noodle, Corning.

Nike's Rise to the Heights

When you think of companies that started out from nothing to become multi-billion-dollar businesses by introducing innovative branded products, Nike stands out. Its story is quite remarkable.

The year was 1964, and Phil Knight, Nike's founder and a graduate of the University of Oregon and Stanford Business School, launched his sports equipment business called BRS (Blue Ribbon Sports) by hawking Tiger running shoes made in

Japan at athletic events from the back of his truck. Soon Knight began making his own shoes and he changed his company's name to Nike—after the winged goddess of victory in Greek mythology. Nike sat at the side of Zeus, the ruler of the Olympic pantheon, in Olympus. Her mystical presence symbolized victorious battles.

Knight got his big break with a new athletic shoe invented by Bill Bauerman, the coach at the University of Oregon. As the story goes, Bauerman put some rubber compound in his wife's waffle iron and baked himself some rubber waffles. He cut them to fit the sole of some shoes and glued them in place. When his athletes tried out the shoes they gave them good reviews for their traction and extra cushioning. Thus was born the Nike waffle trainer—the most innovative athletic shoe in the 1970s—and it put Knight's Nike on the map.

By 1979, Nike was number one in athletic shoe sales and on its way to becoming as popular a U.S. brand as Coca-Cola. When Nike lost that ranking to Reebok, which capitalized on the aerobic craze sweeping across the country at that time, Nike's counterstrategy was to diversify its shoe lines so that it could market footwear specific to any kind of sport or activity. To surpass Reebok, Knight needed another big-time break. He got it when he signed a young Michael Jordan. Fresh out of the University of North Carolina, Jordan was being touted by sports writers as the next Larry Bird. Little did they know that Jordan would single-handedly go on to paint professional basketball the color platinum and become the most recognizable person on planet Earth.

Nike's designers and engineers went to work developing an unconventional shoe for Jordan. The end product was a black-and-red-designed shoe with an innovative pressure air unit in the heel branded Air Jordan. This would prove to create lots of attention for Air Jordans because at that time it was illegal for players to wear black shoes in the NBA. Jordan kept wearing them even though he was fined $1,000 per game. The controversy only fueled the hunger of teenagers and young men to own Nike Air Jordan shoes.

Nike went on to introduce other innovative branded shoes like the Air Pegasus, with a bigger air unit in the heel, Air Max, with a dual pressure air unit in the heel and a large forefoot air unit for greater comfort and durability, and Air Structure offering great stability and full-length air support.

With the combination of innovative products, a great umbrella brand (Nike), the world-famous winglike "swoosh" Nike symbol, attention-getting product brand names like Air Max, high-profile athletes as Nike spokespeople, and brilliant marketing strategies and great advertising campaigns like "Just do it," Knight has truly paid homage to the Greek mythological winged goddess of victory called Nike.

When I think of how Nike in just over two decades built a $4-billion empire on rethinking rubber, I ask myself why is it that the big tire makers like Firestone/Bridgestone, Goodyear, and Michelin haven't been able to find real innovation in tire design and manufacturing? Like a tire that gives a visual or sound signal of some kind to warn the driver that the tire's air pressure is too high or too low.

Yes, product innovation means a giant leap forward in building the omnipowerful brand, but as this book reveals, it takes much more than that. Yet it always amazes me when a marketing chief assumes that a breakthrough product is all the company needs to catapult the product into the realm of marketing stardom. I recall a phone conversation I had some years back with such an executive at a division of Emerson Electric. While he was reluctant to tell me the specifics of his company's new product invention, he made a point of saying that it was the "mousetrap of all mousetraps." The nature of his inquiry was to learn about our process for devising a brand image strategy and creating brand names, as well as to get an idea of our fee structure.

Within three minutes I realized that he didn't have an appreciation for what it takes to develop a great brand name or what the value of a great brand name could be in building sales for his company's new invention. "We would never spend more than a few thousand dollars to develop a brand name," he said. "In fact, we could call this new product 'Cat Dung' and it would sell. It's that good."

"Well," I answered, "if a name like Cat Dung can sell your

new product, imagine how many more sales you could ring up if you called it 'Mink Dung.' "

The lesson here for all companies with established brands is to look for ways to rethink their products in order to add more meat to the bone. This is especially important for those brands that have been losing market share to competitive products and to new arrivals that have made their products more attractive to consumers.

The Unexpected Little Things That Add Up to a Big Brand Statement

My firm's European and Asian clients are always amused at the Hollywood-like productions that American companies put on to make a big brand statement. I reply that often the perception of the brand in the public's mind demands such an elaborate production, such as the gala opening of Planet Hollywood in Las Vegas, attended by many of Hollywood's biggest movie superstars, television and sports celebrities, top fashion models, business moguls, and the international jet set. The Planet Hollywood brand rises above the name of any motion picture superstar—past or present. It captures the image of an exciting dining experience inspired by the worlds of film and television. Each Planet Hollywood dining experience houses some of the most memorable film and television memorabilia in the world (see Figure 9). The restaurant's four principals (Sylvester Stallone, Bruce Willis, Demi Moore, and Arnold Schwarzenegger) are shown in Figure 10.

After all, "the unexpected" is a critical element in the marketing success of many big-name brands like Planet Hollywood, Disney, Nike, Coca-Cola, and Trump. When people visit Atlantic City for the first time they're counting on Donald Trump to dazzle them with his hotel and casino creations—and that's exactly what Trump delivers.

But if you think that the success of the Trump brand is all about show biz, glamor, and big splashes, you're wrong; it's about paying attention to the details, lots of details that add

Figure 9. The Planet Hollywood dining experience.

Courtesy of Planet Hollywood International, Inc.

up to a memorable brand statement. Just walk through the grand lobby of the famed Trump Tower on Fifth Avenue in midtown Manhattan adjacent to the Tiffany building and you'll see what I'm talking about.

The atrium, a six-story open interior, crowned by a transparent skylight in a bronze frame, is graced by terraced walkways, hanging gardens, and a spectacular eighty-foot waterfall constructed of more than 1,000 pieces of sculptured Breccia Pernice marble. (See Figure 11.) The walls and floors are also constructed of the same Italian marble. Ornamental metals, bronze, and lights create a sparkling wall of rolling water that cascades into a series of pools on the garden restaurant level. True to the Trump brand, this residential, retail, and office tower is 664 feet high, making it the tallest residential building and the tallest concrete structure in New York.

Yet history has shown that spending megabucks on a big

Figure 10. Planet Hollywood's four principals.

Courtesy of Planet Hollywood International, Inc.

brand statement doesn't guarantee the brand's success in the marketplace. According to advertising insiders, McDonald's spent $100 million on TV and print media ads for its new Arch Deluxe sandwich and burger just to outdo Microsoft's Windows 95 big splash. A year later, the much touted new brand is expected to be discontinued, according to a 1998 CNN news report. In the same TV segment a Wall Street restaurant analyst noted that the upscale product with a menu price to match was a huge marketing blunder and that McDonald's had to stop trying to be all things to all people and get back to the business of offering value-priced burgers and other popular fast-food items that appeal to its core customers.

From my viewpoint, McDonald's has a better chance of winning back the market share it lost to its rivals Burger King and Wendy's by focusing on those unexpected little things that add up to a big brand statement.

Figure 11. The famed Trump Tower atrium in New York City.

Courtesy of the Trump Organization.

Here's how companies that have built the omnipowerful brand use the four principles of the "unexpected little things" brand strategy to outdistance their competitors.

1. *Stress thoughtfulness.* Insist that all employees be observant of customer needs and that they respond accordingly with an unusual effort.

2. *Be courtesy-driven.* Educate all employees to understand that civility and attentiveness to customers are essential to the company's success, and that they will be rewarded for outstanding service performance.

3. *Emphasize trust.* Teach employees that trust is the foundation of building good customer relationships and that all customers should be viewed as honorable people.

4. *Stick to good business sense.* Create an atmosphere in which all employees can override a general customer service policy if the situation calls for it and common sense says that both the customer and the company will benefit.

While these four principles may seem obvious, the truth is that many companies, including the giants of industry, have forgotten or deliberately discarded some or all of them in the search for profits.

Yet if one examines the *real* reasons for the downfall of many once-famous U.S. brands like Woolworth and Pan Am, among others, you'll probably find that at some critical point in the company's history a newly appointed management team lost sight of those customer service principles that had been the hallmarks of the company's founding fathers. In other cases, where a brand's market share got hammered, you'll probably find a corporate management team that didn't keep a watchful eye over the quality of its customer service performance.

Look at AT&T when this telecommunications giant had a monopoly on local and long-distance telephone service. AT&T's management staffs, personnel, and phone operators were not known for practicing the four principles I've just reviewed. Let's face it, AT&T knew that in the absence of competition it had its customer by the groin.

After the breakup of the company in 1982, a trimmed-down AT&T found itself in a competitive environment for long-distance customers. Faced with the prospect of losing customers to MCI, Sprint, and other new start-ups, AT&T's management staff, personnel, and operators got a crash course in good phone manners. Statements like "Thank you for using AT&T" and "We value your business," rarely heard by AT&T's customers before the breakup, were suddenly in vogue. But for many of AT&T's customers, this overnight shift to the philosophy that the customer is king was too long in coming and they switched to other long-distance carriers.

Since the breakup of the Bell companies, AT&T has easily spent a billion dollars in direct mail promotion, telemarketing, and advertising and PR campaigns in an effort to persuade its lost customers to come back to AT&T long distance.

So, if you're looking for an almost cost-free method of building your brand's image power, "the unexpected little things add up to a big brand statement" marketing strategy is the answer. Actually, a loosely hinged version of this marketing strategy was widely practiced in this country through the first half of the twentieth century by businesses of all types and sizes. But it gradually disappeared thanks to a misguided corporate "time is money" mentality, and being thoughtful, attentive, and courteous to customers requires time and that translates into a loss of profits.

I wasn't around to see this commonsense brand strategy in practice. I experienced it first in Italy in 1985.

The Italian Way

My flight destination from New York was Rome, and soon after arriving at the Excelsior Hotel on via Veneto, I decided to explore the shops on via Condotti, considered by many to be Italy's Rodeo Drive.

I entered Valentino's boutique for men and was greeted warmly by a young salesman. I must have spent an hour in the store, and the salesman stayed with me the whole time as I looked at racks of jackets, suits, pants, and shirts. While there were good buys to be had, I thought it would be wise to visit other Italian brand-name shops in the vicinity before making any major purchases. I thanked the salesman for his patience and time and headed toward the front door only to notice that he was ahead of my footsteps in order to open the door for me. Outside on the sidewalk, he extended his hand and said, "Have a pleasant stay in Rome and if I can be of help to recommend a good local restaurant for dinner, please don't hesitate to come back and I'll call the restaurant to make a reservation for you."

"What's so unusual about this?" a European might ask. Well, as an American consumer, I was taken by complete surprise by this salesman's thoughtfulness and courtesy. Whether you live in New York, Los Angeles, Seattle, Houston, Chicago, or Atlanta, getting a salesman in a department store or men's shop at noontime to spend five uninterrupted minutes with you is nothing short of a miracle, and if you're not handing him your credit card by that time, he's unlikely to be seen again. And the thought of his leaving his sacred turf to escort a customer all the way to the store's front door, let alone offering to be of assistance to a customer who has made no purchase, just doesn't happen every day in any major city in the United States.

"Well," I thought, "this can't be the norm. I just happened to find a salesman in Rome with old-fashioned good manners." I would soon learn after visiting other shops that "When in Rome, this is what the Romans do."

I next headed to Brioni's flagship men's store whose manager, Sergio, I had met some weeks earlier at Brioni's New York shop on Park Avenue and 52nd Street. He was expecting a visit from me.

After the typically warm Italian reception—followed by an espresso forte, of course—Sergio showed me Brioni's new men's lines. An hour later, Sergio was writing a sales receipt for the two suits, two sports jackets, six pairs of dress slacks, and nine ties that I had selected. "Sergio," I remarked, "I am leaving Rome in three days for Positano on the Amalfi coast and I realize that's not enough time for you to have my pants and suits altered."

"The alterations will be done at no cost by our New York store's tailor when you return to Manhattan," he said and then called the manager of the store in my presence to confirm this understanding. "Everything has been arranged. I will have your clothes wrapped and delivered to your hotel this evening."

After I was led to the front door by Sergio and we stood together outside Brioni's, I said, *"Grazie mille!"*

"Prego! Prendersi una buona vacanza a Positano," he replied as we shook hands. What followed next would make for an extremely funny skit on cultural differences. At the same time, it was an example of how unusual effort on the part of everyday employees helps to build a company's brand into the omnipowerful brand in the customer's mind.

About a block away, I heard Sergio call out my name. I turned to look and he was still standing outside the store's entrance. His arm was raised high and I could see the palm of his hand waving back and forth in a good-bye gesture. At the next traffic light, I again heard Sergio calling my name. This time he was standing a block away at the street's intersection waving good-bye. I returned the gesture and continued walking. A short distance from the hotel, I heard Sergio calling out to me a third time. I turned and sure enough there he was waving goodbye.

Now, two thoughts ran through my mind: Either Sergio was mentally disturbed, or I, the naive American tourist, had paid far more than any Roman would have paid for the same clothes and he couldn't thank me enough for the big sales commission he was earning.

Sergio finally caught up with me. Out of breath, he asked, "Il signor Delano, why do you continue to walk away when I motion with my hand for you to come to me?"

When I explained to him that his hand signal in the United States means good-bye, not come here, we both broke into laughter. He soon came to the point of his frantic waving: "You forgot to take your sales receipt and you'll need this for American customs." He then handed me a small envelope.

This extraordinary thoughtfulness and courtesy to customers, which I found throughout my travels in Italy, is as much a part of the Italian business culture as the daily pasta dish. Ordinary people working in hotels, shops, cafés, and salons greet you with salutations of *"Buon giorno"* and *"Buona sera."* As I reflect back on this, it's a sad commentary on our American business culture that such simple greetings as "Good day" and "Good evening" are rarely heard or given by people in our nation's workforce today.

In Positano, I stayed at Le Sirenuse. If one adds up all the little things that this hotel provides for its guests, you'll understand why it's rated among the world's top ten hotels. But what stands out most in my mind about this family-owned hostelry can be distilled into one word: *trust.* For starters, when you arrive at the hotel, you're not asked to complete a guest registration form or have your American Express card imprinted. If the hotel is expecting you, announcing your name is all it takes to find yourself moments later in a suite overlooking the Mediterranean Sea. If you dine at the hotel's restaurant, have drinks at the pool, request a Havana cigar, or receive room service, there's never a room bill to sign. Remembering the names and faces of its guests is how the hotel's staff manages to keep track of everything with an unusually high degree of accuracy. And it's this feeling of trust that makes the hotel's guests feel as if they're staying at their own private villa, not at a commercially run hotel.

Another little touch that adds to this feeling is the absence of hotel-like directional signs mounted on walls pointing the way to the lobby, rest rooms, dining room, bar, pool, outdoor terrace, and so on. With a ratio of almost one hotel employee for every two guests, the service is extraordinary.

Unexpected Service With a Smile

For companies that are service-oriented, like banks, brokerage houses, supermarkets, department stores, airlines, automotive dealerships, and hotel and restaurant chains, among others, implementing this strategy is all about changing employees' attitudes toward the customer—training them to look for

rhea faster than six spoonfuls of the pink stuff (Pepto-Bismol) has *powerbat* marketing potential to build your brand.

7. *Credibility.* "Make it believable" is stressed several times in this book whether it's in the creation of a brand name, a brand slogan, or a personal sales letter, among other media. It also holds true for an advertisement. If your advertising's selling idea or execution sounds a false note, the consumer will immediately become suspicious. Great ads go to the edge of believability, but they never cross that line; therein lies their magic.

Again, if you have followed my firm's proven process for creating a great brand name, you have acquired a wealth of information about your new brand to share with your ad agency. At this point, you have:

- Determined what is the most compelling story about your new brand that you wish to communicate.
- Targeted your new brand's prime buyers or users.
- Gained insights into your competition's brands—specifically, the thrust of their image positioning stance in the marketplace.
- Determined your new brand's correct sexual profile (Total Feminine, A-feminine, A-sexual, A-masculine, or Total Masculine) and have selected the correct image positioning zone for your brand on the Image Map.
- Identified the do's and don'ts guiding all creative development.
- Defined your new brand's character, personality, and product heritage.

In short, you have established a number of well-defined yardsticks by which to measure the intellectual and creative execution of the advertisement your agency develops for your new or existing brand. And you should be able to spot immediately an ad that is irrelevant to the product's selling proposition, directed to the wrong buyer profile and demographics, lacking in freshness and originality, or off track with the brand's character, personality, and product legacy, all of which can be devastating to your advertisement.

The Need for a Compelling Story and Much More

Nothing else is so important to the success of your advertisement as your decision as to what is the most compelling story to tell about your brand-name product. While brand positioning needs to be precisely articulated and targeted to the prime buyer audience, the product's most compelling story usually speaks to one of these three themes: the product's essence, the product's uniqueness, or the product's spirit. If you make a strategic mistake here by selecting a theme that is not focused on your product's most compelling story, you'll have missed out on the opportunity to develop a *powerbat* advertisement, and there's a good chance that your advertising will derail your brand's growth.

How do you decide what is the most compelling product story to tell in your brand's advertisement? It's rather simple when you consider the options. If your product has a unique selling proposition or a unique product story that no competitor can tell, then focus on that uniqueness. If your product by its very uplifting spirit will enhance the buyer's lifestyle or change his perceptions of himself in a positive way, then focus on that spirit. If the sum and substance of the product is the most compelling story to tell, then focus on that essence.

In some cases, the product's most compelling story will relate to more than one theme. For example, "headache relief" is the sum and substance of the brand Excedrin. Yet headache relief is also the product's unique selling proposition as compared to other over-the-counter medicines that are advertised as a remedy for a variety of ailments. To ensure that you've made the right call, ask yourself: "Does the product theme selected speak to the overriding reason that sold you on investing a fortune to bring this product into the marketplace?" If it does, now you need your ad agency to come up with a big idea that fully captures your brand's most compelling story.

Making the Big Idea a Memorable Brand Image That's All Your Own

One way to build brand recognition through your advertisement is to find or invent a memorable brand image (symbol or character) that's all your own. Some of these images have become marketing *powerbats*. Just look at how the Energizer pink bunny added high octane to a product line that most people never think about until they need replacement batteries.

Here's a quick test to see if you can correctly identify the companies responsible for these familiar advertised product images:

1. What brand commercial shows a pin landing on a tabletop next to a phone handset?
   (a) AT&T   (b) MCI   (c) Sprint
2. What brand commercial opens with computer-animation polar bears on a glacier?
   (a) Pepsi-Cola   (b) Seven-Up   (c) Coca-Cola
3. What brand commercial tells you to look for Juan Valdez on the package?
   (a) Goya   (b) Chiquita   (c) The National Federation of Coffee Growers of Colombia

The answers will be revealed as you read on.

Sprint's challenge was to find an advertising product symbol that would demonstrate the superior sound clarity of its fiber optic telephone lines compared with the conventional lines used by its main competitor, AT&T. The solution: A simple hemming pin. Sprint's advertisement proved to Americans that a person could hear a pin drop while listening on the other end of the phone if they were connected to Sprint's long-distance fiber optic network.

Coca-Cola's marketing dugout is brimming with *powerbat* brand images—the Coca-Cola script logo design; the Coca-Cola Classic, Coke, and Diet Coke brand names; the Coca-Cola red color; the original Coke glass bottle shape; the brand's white swirl design inspired by that same bottle's distinctive shape and featured prominently on bottle labels, cans, cartons, soda dispensing machines, and trucks. So, what new advertising image could possibly top these famous brand images to further build the taste for Coca-Cola refreshment? The answer: computer-animated polar bears that belch after downing a big bottle of Coke in a few gulps. By the way, the Coca-Cola stuffed polar bears are among the hottest-selling items in the company's brand stores.

The compelling product story in the commercial for The Federation of Coffee Growers of Colombia is this: You're buying the best coffee beans in the world. To guarantee that all coffee aficionados are indeed buying 100 percent Colombian coffee, the advertised trademark of Juan Valdez standing next to his mule appears on the product's packaging.

Making the Advertised Image Consistent With Your Umbrella Brand's Image

If the image you select for your advertised product is inconsistent with the image of your company's umbrella brand, you could be putting both your product and your umbrella brand in real jeopardy. Whimsical brand characters like the Coca-Cola polar bears and the Energizer bunny work because their corporate umbrella brands are positioned to appeal to the "Mainstream Buyer" in the middle zone of the Image Map. When a corporate umbrella brand's positioning is in the top or second zone of the Image Map, to go after buyers of "Premium-Priced" and "Status Label" products with a children's playtime character can be a costly mistake.

While there are plenty of past examples with which to make my case, I found a recent example in the September 8, 1997, issue of *Advertising Age*. The excerpted quotations from the article titled "Catera's daffy duck ads don't fly," by Rance Crain, the editor-in-chief of this respected international advertising weekly journal, say it all.

To set the stage, the article sounded a wake-up call to auto companies who become mesmerized when awareness of their brand-name vehicles is on the rise. Crain reminded them that a higher level of awareness often doesn't translate into higher sales. The article quoted a researcher who told *Automotive News* that the Cadillac Catera ads raised awareness among young buyers. But, he said, "Getting people to buy [the Catera] is another story."

Crain noted that the Catera continues to be saddled with Cadillac's fuddy-duddy image. "So far, Catera's daffy ads starring a duck have missed their target audience," he said. "Catera has mainly attracted Cadillac and other GM shoppers." According to Crain, Catera has an impossible row to hoe because all other Cadillac models are aimed at the over-sixty crowd. "So, is it any wonder that Catera missed the baby boom market?" asks Crain.

Getting to the heart of the issue, he said, "When baby boomers see the ads for Catera, duck or no duck, their awareness of Catera might be heightened, but they won't buy a Catera because they have been preconditioned to believe the Cadillac brand is not for them."

But his most stinging statement came at the end: "The Catera is not, and never will be, a Cadillac. It could be an upscale Saturn, but as a Cadillac, it's destined to join Cimarron and Allante in the Cadillac graveyard."

Giving Your Product's Features a Three-Dimensional Edge

A good example is the commercial for the GMC Yukon. To make the point that you've got a commanding view when you're behind the wheel of this awesome full-size utility vehicle, the view from the Yukon in the commercial looks down the side of a towering building to the street below. To show that the Yukon has more cargo space than any other vehicle in its class, the commercial shows suitcases tumbling one after the other into the rear compartment of the Yukon from an airport-like baggage conveyor ramp.

Focusing on Another Compelling Theme When Your Product's Selling Feature Is Obvious

A great number of brand advertisements are downright boring because the message is focused on an obvious selling feature of the product. How many times do we have to be reminded in Weight Watchers commercials that the product it's selling is weight loss? Two different dietetic brands offer lessons on how to find a new advertising theme that's even more compelling than the product's original selling proposition.

We all know that Nabisco's SnackWell's are dietetic cookies. To keep talking about "low fat" in the product's commercials is no longer a compelling message. Not surprisingly, SnackWell's has launched a new ad campaign. The commercial breaks new ground for a cookie product. The steamy scene of a couple clad in skimpy bathing attire making out on a sandy beach could easily be mistaken for a Calvin Klein Obsession fragrance commercial. But aside from the sexual overtones, the advertising theme is focused on passion and desire. And since there's less fat to worry about with SnackWell's cookies, "Why not indulge in life's pleasures?" is the message of this new *powerbat* TV spot.

The very brand name Diet Coke tells us that this is a "low calorie" soft drink. Even if *diet* didn't appear in the name, it wouldn't take long for consumers to figure out what the product's feature is. To create an advertisement that mentions or even alludes to a dietetic product would result in an ad that's talking to itself. Being an astute marketer, Coca-Cola positioned its Diet Coke brand as a *great* cola taste, not specifically as a *diet* cola. I submit that "Just for the taste of it" is one of the best ad theme lines in the annals of American advertising, and the individual or individuals who crafted these memorable six words deserve to receive a million-dollar-plus bonus from the Coca-Cola Company. After all, if Michael Jordan deserves to earn an estimated ten thousand dollars each time he bounces a basketball on the court in an official game, what's a million or two to the people who helped to make Diet Coke a billion-dollar global sales success?

Where a Great Brand Name Pays Off

A great brand name can tell you more about the image appropriateness of a print ad or TV spot than an eighty-page document detailing the brand's strategic positioning. If your brand name seems out of place with your product's ad, there's a good chance that your ad will be a costly failure.

A great brand name also adds a distinctive personality to the product's advertisement. By contrast, a misery brand name can make an ad with lots of glamor and visual impact fall flat on its face. The TV spot for the RL, a luxury Acura sedan, is a prime example. The spot opens with a copy line on the screen that says in essence "Here's the new RL." Right there, in those first critical seconds of the commercial, the car's brand personality is expressed in two letters that are about as inviting as a pair of wet socks.

The Pitfalls of Reactionary Advertising

What you want to avoid at all cost is what I call reactionary advertising. We often see such knee-jerk responses when a brand's market share is under downward pressure or, worse yet, in a nosedive. Instead of asking what the brand's most compelling story is and then executing an ad with a big idea that fully captures it by way of a provocative theme line, the agency struggles to find a new advertising slant in the hope that it will boost the brand's market share ranking. Too often these new ads created out of a sense of desperation only add to more market share hemorrhaging because the focus is still on an irrelevant product theme, not a powerful message about the brand. GM Oldsmobile's advertising comes to mind.

Taking Advantage of a Brand's Legacy

For the year ending 1997, Oldsmobile's total unit sales dropped to a number that the GM division once set in 1961, a time when Volkswagen Beetle ads were telling consumers to "Think Small" and it was a rarity to see a BMW or a Datsun Japanese-made car on U.S. roads. So, what's causing Oldsmobile's marketing woes and declining market share? Some ex-Oldsers told me that management didn't push the envelope far enough when it ordered the redesign of the division's products and that it listened too much to the opinions of consumers rather than to GM's design and engineering captains. Some outsiders said that Oldsmobile has to reposition its brand image from that of being a stodgy, old-person's car by way of new products and new branding. Other insiders put the blame on management's decision to hand over the marketing reins to people with no proven brand-building track record when Oldsmobile was at a critical juncture in the late 1980s. But one thing all these people agreed on is that the automaker's advertising has been—and continues to be—reactionary and execution-driven rather than focused on a compelling story that clearly separates Oldsmobile's umbrella brand from its rivals.

There are important lessons here to be learned by all companies regardless of their industry. And they especially apply to those companies that have a *legitimate* and *rich* product history and now find themselves in the eye of a marketing hurricane.

Let me return to a point I made earlier about selecting an advertising theme: If you have a unique story that no competitor can tell, then focus on that uniqueness. If you look at Oldsmobile's advertising in recent years, you will see that the product theme has focused on vehicles that offer a "unique selling proposition." Yet that's a real hard sell and here's why. For every Oldsmobile product that's advertised, there are at least a dozen competing products, domestic and foreign, in the same price range that offer as good as or even better design and engineering features, comfort, safety, and road handling performance. So, the logical question is: Why is Oldsmobile's management staying with a product advertising theme that isn't working when it has a unique story to tell?

Here's another problem facing Oldsmobile: Most buyers of upscale products are naturally hesitant to purchase any brand that's lost significant market share to its competitors. Just look at Apple Computer. Only a decade ago, its line of Macintosh PCs commanded a prime location in retail computer outlets. Now, with its market share battered and beaten down, you have to search the back aisles of a computer store to find one Macintosh demo.

Ironically, Oldsmobile has a free ticket to a *powerbat* advertising theme and a brand positioning strategy that many of its rivals can only dream about. The free ticket I am referring to is called *brand legacy.* Brand legacy is by far and away the automaker's most compelling story, and it's an impressive one at that. For starters, who else can boast that it's the first and only American automaker to celebrate one hundred years of doing business? That it was the first to forge a path in automotive engineering and design that Detroit's other car makers would follow? That the Oldsmobile Curved Dash was the first mass-produced car in America? That the Oldsmobile Starfire Convertible was hailed as a breakthrough in automotive styling when it made its debut in 1955? And that the powertrain in the Oldsmobile Rocket 88 had no equal in its day?

Yet, instead of reminding consumers of its glorious automotive history, Oldsmobile actually distanced itself from its brand heritage in 1988 with a much-ridiculed ad theme line that said: "This is *not* your father's Oldsmobile." And many consumers—including loyal Oldsers—interpreted that theme line as being an apology for having made inferior cars in the past.

When Oldsmobile celebrated its centennial anniversary in late August 1997, CNN reported on the event. The TV segment showed the first car made by the Olds company in 1897. It went on to show other vintage Oldsmobile brand-name cars and concluded with Aurora and the stylish Intrigue (the latter hailed by some auto analysts as GM's best mid-size cars). CNN also noted some of the company's automotive design and engineering accomplishments. Following the segment, the CNN news co-anchor in his mid-sixties said that when he was growing up his father owned Oldsmobile cars exclusively. His co-anchor in her mid-thirties remarked that she had no idea that Oldsmobile had such a rich automotive history. And her comment goes to the crux of Oldsmobile's umbrella brand image problem. It's only reasonable to conclude that tens of millions of other Americans in their twenties, thirties, forties, and fifties are unaware of the car company's brand legacy; so why Oldsmobile continues not to find an effective and imaginative way to weave in its brand legacy in its advertising is simply mind-boggling.

While Oldsmobile's sales are declining, Mercedes-Benz

sales in North America are exceeding expectations. The auto-maker's product legacy happens to be the theme of one of five new commercials created by Lowe & Partners/SMS, New York. As we watch archival footage from the 1950s up to the present day of people racing, driving, building, polishing, or just ad-miring their Mercedes-Benz cars in driveways or winner's cir-cles, every scene features the people singing "Falling in Love Again." The spot, according to *Ad Age* critic Bob Garfield, uses genuine historical footage, digitally matted, and new material shot with antique equipment. "This magnificent achievement in special-effects understatement is an eloquent reminder of our enduring love affair with the car," stated Garfield. The spot closes with the line "Come fall in love again."

Personally, I can't think of another auto company that has done so much to keep its brand and product heritage alive in consumers' minds. Go to an auto show and you'll likely find vintage Mercedes-Benz cars parked side by side with the auto-maker's current lineup of vehicles and tomorrow's prototypes. The message conveyed here is quite powerful: This brand is steeped in traditional values in having always built cars boast-ing a unique combination of luxury, high performance, styling, and heritage. Yet, as Garfield noted, the new advertising spots created by the Lowe agency yield an equally unique combina-tion of passion, prestige, romance, and fun. "The consequence is the finest car campaign on the air, and the best Mercedes advertising ever done," he said.

Bridging the past with the present to underscore a tradi-tion of excellence is also the theme of an American Airlines TV commercial. And in the words of Ayer two decades ago, it's the kind of advertising that makes human contact.

It all starts with a spot in a plane maintenance hangar, where a burly-looking chief mechanic in his early sixties says, "Oh well, I never thought about retiring. . . ." We learn that it's his last day on the job after some thirty-six years as a mechanic with American Airlines.

"Years ago we relied on hand tools to get the job done," he says as the scene changes and we see rows of red tool boxes in a plane hangar from yesteryear.

The scene shifts back to the present and we see mechanics

with high-tech devices in their hands checking for defects on a wide-body fuselage. "Well," he adds, "today we use ultrasound to check for microscopic voids and x-rays . . . magnetic imaging. . . ." Then the message of a brand legacy built on the efforts of ordinary people hits home when the mechanic says, "The tools have changed but the job hasn't."

The mechanic goes on to announce, "We're not just responsible for these planes, we're responsible for the people that fly in them. . . . I'm proud to say that for the past thirty-six years, I've been part of that." In the last scene the chief mechanic receives a surprise ovation from his fellow workers. We come away thinking we know this guy, he's a real person—he could be our father, uncle, or next-door neighbor. More important, we realize that passenger safety has always been a top priority for this global carrier. Brand advertising just doesn't get any better than this, and the people responsible for creating and executing these commercials each deserve to receive a check in the amount of one million dollars, if not more, from American Airlines.

Attitude-Driven Advertising That Builds the Brand

The best way to learn how advertising builds the brand is to study Nike's ad campaigns and its swoosh brand marketing strategy. Why? Because Nike takes the gold hands down over *all* other marketers out there for its brand-building know-how via advertising. A decade ago, Nike's attitude was that it was going to be number one in athletic footwear and an apparel giant. The Nike ads that followed featuring compelling theme lines like "Just do it" presented the same winning attitude to the public. There are many reasons Nike's advertising has an endless power to surprise. Here are four of them:

1. First and foremost, it embodies the very heart and spirit of sports.
2. It's all about big-name athletes and exposure.
3. It speaks to product innovation.
4. Competitors haven't put up much of an ad challenge,

perhaps because they're intimidated by Nike's *power-bat* advertising campaigns.

While Volvo Cars of North America's advertising shifts to reposition the Volvo brand as more fun, it's not about to abandon the safety image it has built up over three decades of advertising. Its latest $35-million national ad campaign for its first U.S. all-wheel-drive station wagons assumes that the new Volvo V70 Cross Country is the safest vehicle on the road. In the voice-over, actor Donald Sutherland says, "It is perhaps our most impressive safety advance ever—a Volvo that can save your soul." The three TV spots shot in New Zealand show the Cross Country vehicles with their owners down-hill skiing, kayaking, and mountain biking.

What strikes me about Volvo's brand advertising is that it's totally attitude-driven. By that I mean I can't recall seeing one advertisement from Volvo that explains how the design of its vehicles can actually save your life in a highway crash. And its new Cross Country TV spots say nothing about how this station wagon can save your soul. A current Saab TV spot makes the comparison that all Saab vehicles are equipped with four-wheel drive, whereas only one Volvo model can make that particular claim of product safety. Yet, ask people what is a safe family vehicle to own, and the brand Volvo is certain to be mentioned.

Chanel ads take the position that anything branded Chanel is chic; M&M/Mars Snickers candy bar ads take the position that a Snickers is what you should grab when there's no real food around; Boston Market ads take the position that you shouldn't mess with dinner because they offer traditional comfort food at reasonable prices; and Celestial Seasonings ads take the position that its teas will give women moments of contemplative solitude.

What these advertisements have in common is this: a winning brand attitude. For such attitude-driven ads, often there are no hard data or scientific proof to support the product's implied benefit to the consumer. Yet they can be immensely successful because people gravitate to ads that position the brand with certainty, not vagueness. These attitude-driven ads can't be quantified in words or neatly packaged into five or seven steps explaining how it's done. It's nothing more than an attitude that a company takes about its brand. A word of caution, however: The success of an attitude-driven print ad or TV commercial depends on an above-average product and a brand message that doesn't cross the line of believability.

What Advertising Can and Cannot Do

A false assumption held by many corporate executives is that a great advertisement can build any brand. True, there's always that unexpected great advertisement that catapults a brand into momentary stardom. But for a brand to rise to stardom and remain there for years and even decades, it takes excellence in brand management over a wide range of fronts.

The role of advertising is to make the target buying audience aware of the advertised product, to do a certain amount of preselling of the product, and to motivate interested parties to take the next step of learning more about the product. But as Rance Crain noted earlier, there's no guarantee that building awareness of the product through advertising will translate into higher sales. On the other hand, the sales outcome of certain product impulse-driven ads is almost predictable down to the dollar. A week before Valentine's Day, a Tiffany print ad in leading business journals for an Elsa Peretti "Open Heart" pendant on a 30-inch chain in 18-karat gold or sterling silver will result in sales of these jewelry pieces that have already been calculated by Tiffany from prior years' sales data.

Here's another thing to take into consideration. Advertising on the airwaves is no longer the powerful medium it was in the 1960s and 1970s to build the brand. Unless your product's TV spots appear on six or more of the most frequently watched network cable programs, your advertising is not going to be effective.

And if your company is growing and you see a regional or national advertising campaign as a logical next step to reach more target buyers, keep this thought in mind: Advertising is like Upjohn's Rogaine hair regrowth product; if you stop using it, you'll see no benefit. So, unless your company is prepared to be an advertiser on a regular basis, it might be better to look at other media options like direct mail to reach prospective buyers and users of your brand-name products.

When Ad Sloganeering Works to Build the Brand

Why is it that CEOs have such a passion for brand catch-phrases? Could it be that they regard the brand painting as incomplete without the frame? Many advertising executives would argue that signing off on a TV spot or print ad with just the brand's name is unthinkable; you need a slogan under the ad's signature to help build brand awareness with consumers. Now, here's the shocker: You can count on one hand the brand slogans that the average person can remember. This means that all those thousands of brand slogans out there in the marketplace are not only ineffective, they may well be building the competition's brand or someone else's brand since most people can't recall which brand slogan belongs to what company. These are precisely the findings of my firm's testing of hundreds of brand slogans with thousands of consumers over the past three years.

Here's a quick test (Part I): Do you know the brands behind the advertised slogans *a* through *i* below? Keep in mind that I've selected slogans that are advertised nationally on television and in leading business magazines and journals. All the brands that these catchphrases represent are in the big leagues; some are number one in their industry.

a. "It's all within your reach."
b. "You've got a friend in the business."
c. "What you never thought possible."
d. "We're there when you need us."
e. "The power of partnership."
f. "A tradition of trust."
g. "The relentless pursuit of perfection."
h. "The way the world works."
i. "We bring good things to life."

The answers are given at the end of this chapter.

Don't feel dumb if you're having difficulty; most business-people and consumers with whom we conducted this test failed miserably. Either they associated the wrong brand with the slogan (often a brand in a totally different industry) or they were at a total loss. Example *i* had better recall than the others because of the big advertising dollars this advertiser has spent over the past decade building this brand slogan.

Now, here's Part II of this quick test: Do you know the brands behind the advertising slogans *j* through *m* below?

j. "The ultimate driving machine."
k. "This Bud's for you."
l. "The Museum Watch."
m. "Good to the last drop."

Unless you've been away from planet Earth for some time, you should know the brands behind these four slogans above; most people in our test did. Now, why is it that almost every respondent in our brand slogan test failed Part I but passed Part II with flying colors?

Well, the answer should be obvious. The first seven brand slogans in the Part I quick test could apply to all the Fortune 1000 companies as well as to a thousand other mid-size companies dotting the American landscape. Take the first slogan: "It's all within your reach." What company believes its products or services are not within its customers' reach? Then the second: "You've got a friend in the business." What company believes it's not your friend in business? Then the third is "What you never thought possible." What company doesn't hold to this philosophy? Then the fourth: "We're there when you need us." What company is foolish enough not to be there when its customers need it? Then the fifth: "The power of partnership." What company thinks it can survive without partnerships with its people, dealers, agencies, suppliers, and so on? Then we have "A tradition of trust." What company believes it has no history of trust? Next comes: "The relentless pursuit of perfection." What big-league company out there is not aggressively looking for ways to perfect its products or services? Then the eighth: "The way the world works." What successful global company today isn't contributing to the way the world works? It's only in the last slogan, "We bring good things to life," that the list of possibilities gets narrowed down. But then again, there are hundreds of other companies in a variety of industries that could make this same claim, and that's where the confusion came in for many of our test respondents.

Come on, let's get serious here; these are all generalized platitudes, not custom-tailored brand slogans; each fits the description of countless companies and their brands. These slogans don't build the advertiser's brand; they build all brands in all industries.

Now, let's look at the three slogans in the Part II quick test. How many auto brands can boast of being "The ultimate driving machine"? Perhaps several could make that claim, but BMW would certainly be on that roster. How many brands could tout "This Bud's for you"? Only one that I know of—Budweiser Beer. How many watch brands can say they are "The Museum Watch"? Movado certainly comes to mind. How many brands remind us that they are "Good to the last drop?" If you said Maxwell House Coffee, you're right.

What's the lesson here? The creators of brand catchphrases need to focus on theme lines that capture the identity of the company's brand head-on. Otherwise, you might as well say in your print ads and TV commercials that your brand theme line "is dedicated to the American free enterprise system." For instance, if your brand slogan identifies the "high-quality standards" or the "unique value" of your product lines, as in "The ultimate driving machine," "The Museum Watch," and "Good to the last drop," you've helped consumers to narrow down to just a few brands that could possibly fit this description. If the Lexus brand slogan had one adjective (*automotive*), how many other brands out there could say "The relentless pursuit of automotive perfection"? ADM's theme line, "Supermarket to the world," is a good competence statement because who else could make this claim? Nissan's "Enjoy the ride" is another example of a good brand theme because how many other car makers can say that their products are "fun to drive"? But perhaps the most brilliant brand slogan of this last quarter century is Nike's "Just do it!" How many other brands can say, "Get off that couch and get physical?"

You can also eliminate any confusion in the consumer's mind by incorporating your brand's name in your ad slogan. The genius who came up with the brilliant brand slogan "This Bud's for you" deserves to receive a million-dollar bonus check from Anheuser-Busch. In just four simple words, we get both a good hint of the beer brand (Budweiser) that's behind this slogan and the message that we're getting something special that only this brand can deliver. Merrill Lynch uses the brand theme line "The difference is Merrill Lynch" in its TV spots. Now, who's going to forget the brand that's behind this catchphrase?

Most CEOs would never think of designing their corporation's logo; that they leave to the talent and skill of graphic designers and advertising people trained in the visual arts. But when it comes to devising a catchphrase that speaks to their company's mission, vision, or rallying motto, it's a different story. After all, the CEO reasons, who else knows the organization's direction better than the person at the helm? And since slogans are built from words, not visual images, the task seems highly feasible for a CEO to accomplish—especially if he or she has a flair for ornate prose. Although I am certain many CEOs wished they had never taken on such a challenge. Why? Because capturing the essence, uniqueness, and spirit of what a company is all about in three, four, or five words can consume months and even a year or more of their time. It also takes a specialized talent and skill, and the CEO would be wise to turn this task over to a proven brand sloganeer.

You may have gotten the impression that I am not an advocate of brand slogans. Quite the contrary, I share the view of many top advertising executives that a print ad or TV commercial needs an ending theme line to frame the advertised message. But that ending theme line, catchphrase, slogan, competence statement, or whatever you want to call it has to build the company's brand and speak only to that company's brand. The good news is that it can be done.

Finally, here are the answers to the Part I quick test:

a. AT&T
b. Gateway Computers
c. Motorola
d. Ryder Trucks
e. Zurich-American Insurance Group
f. Merrill Lynch
g. Lexus
h. FedEx
i. GE

9

The Next Dimension in Power Brand Marketing

The ultimate goal of every company is to have its brand anointed as the one to buy. After all, once consumers have bonded with a brand, it's heaven for a manufacturer as long as it doesn't make a gross marketing blunder or a competitor doesn't come out with a far superior mousetrap.

While no one will argue with this goal, in the next dimension of power brand marketing the new challenge is to make the brand more valuable to the consumer than the original product that put it on the nation's map—the objective being to give the brand a *free agent* status, or the ability to endorse a wide range of consumer products. These are the brands that will be the big winners in the twenty-first century. If you're looking for examples of such brands today, here are three of them—Coca-Cola, Mickey Mouse, and Martha Stewart.

A Brand That Transcends the Product

The one thing you can't buy at The Coca-Cola Store in midtown Manhattan is the "Real Thing." That's right, even on a hot summer's day, there's no ice-cold Coke to gulp down to quench your thirst. The Disney Store isn't selling Mickey Mouse vintage cartoons and comic books on its main shopping floor. It's selling everything else under its Mickey Mouse flagship brand like children's clothes, shampoos, towels, writing paper, wallpaper, you name it. At Kmart stores, you won't find Martha Stewart's first book, *Entertaining* (published in 1982 by Clarkson Potter Inc.), which has nearly 600,000 copies in print and literally set the stage for the Martha Stewart Living brand. But what you will find is Martha Stewart Everyday—a branded design program offering a full line of bed and bath products and a branded line of paints for the home called Martha Stewart Everyday Colors (256 colors) manufactured by Sherwin-Williams.

How do you transform your company's umbrella brand or flagship brands into a tangible asset that consumers want to own? If you're looking for six easy steps, there *are* none because what works for Disney, Planet Hollywood, and Nike will not work for all companies. However, for companies that have accomplished this amazing feat, we have identified certain predictable characteristics that go beyond great advertising and PR campaigns, memorable graphics, package and retail environmental design, outstanding customer service, and products that offer the consumer value for the price. Here are six of them:

1. *They're action-oriented.* These companies don't allow great marketing ideas to be drained of their life juices by having a small army of executives spend a year analyzing their pros and cons and then spending six more months producing a 300-page antiseptic report which in turn is massaged by various corporate staffs, outside consultants, and others for several more months. Instead, they form a special team with fewer than a dozen members which in one or two weeks makes a recommendation to go or not to go with specific brand marketing ideas. And if it's a go, these companies "Just do it," to borrow Nike's famous ad theme line.

2. *They have a vision.* These companies have a vision of where their brand is capable of going. Let's look at a hypotheti-

cal model to drive this point home: Companies A and B both make a premium barbecue sauce that's sold under a distinctive brand name. Each brand is well known throughout the world's major markets. Yet these companies have a different vision of what it means to take their brand to the next dimension in power brand marketing. Company A thinks it's pushing the brand's envelope by introducing new product line extensions like mango- and cilantro-flavored barbecue sauces. Company B, on the other hand, recognizes that its flagship brand is capable of transcending the original sauce that made it a universally known word. So it launches and licenses for marketing a broad range of products associated with barbecue cooking and an American Western lifestyle—products like indoor and outdoor gas and electric grills, patio furniture, steak knives, table settings and linens, poster art, cooking utensils and aprons, jeans, belts, boots, pantry storage shelving, and so forth. And all these products are marketed under the company's famous barbecue sauce brand name.

3. *They focus on their umbrella brand.* These companies focus on building the image power of their umbrella brand because they know that many of the products they sell today will be outdated in a few years or they could be discontinued owing to lagging sales or changes in corporate strategies. For these companies, their umbrella brand is as sacred as their famous flagship brands. Case in point: What would the Mickey Mouse flagship brand be without the Disney umbrella brand endorsing it?

4. *They deliver the unexpected.* These companies continually surprise us with their ability to launch new products and merchandising concepts that expand the horizon of their umbrella brand. Some recent examples: Planet Hollywood comes into our living room with "The Planet Hollywood Game." Martha Stewart introduces "Martha By Mail"—unique merchandise now available online. The online store contains more than sixty products beautifully displayed in three sizes; the Web site visitor is free to browse, and the shopping features created make ordering easy and secure. Nike, with an eye toward the future, launches a stand-alone Jordan brand named

for basketball superstar Michael Jordan. Even though the Jordan products—consisting of a basketball shoe, cross-trainers, and apparel—are swooshless, target buyers, the media, and Wall Street clearly see the Nike brand behind this collection.

5. *They kick the brand up a notch.* To borrow a phrase coined by chef Emeril Lagasse on the TV Food Network's *Emeril Live* show, these companies "kick it up a notch." By this I mean that they know how and when to add the spices, flavors, and heat to make their brands more stylish, appetizing, and sexier than their competitors' brands. Whether you love or hate Martha Stewart, this enterprising woman has built Martha Stewart Living into a powerhouse brand with her "kick it up a notch" home decorating and gardening tips.

6. *They keep their umbrella brand name simple.* These companies—both for profit and nonprofit—have built strong brand awareness by adopting simple and easy-to-remember umbrella brand names in their advertising and all other media communications. It's Disney, not Walt Disney; it's Sears, not Sears, Roebuck; it's Chase, not Chase Manhattan; it's Mobil, not Mobil Oil; it's MoMA, not the Museum of Modern Art to countless millions of people around the world.

Envisioning a Winner

There are thousands of American companies out there in mostly nonglamorous businesses that have the potential to catapult their umbrella brand or flagship brands to global marketing stardom. Stanley Works, based in New Britain, Connecticut, is one such company in my opinion. Why? Because the brand's image lags behind its reality.

Stanley Works is the world's largest manufacturer of hand tools. In addition to its worldwide sales of Stanley Tools and Goldblatt masonry tools, it manufactures and sells regional brands throughout the world. These include Mosley-Stone and Friess paint application products in Europe, Rabone and Goldenberg hand tools also in Europe, and Collins agricultural tools in Latin America.

But the company is more than hand tools today. Its North American Operations are marketing mirror closet doors and surround hardware, decorative wall mirrors, and closet storage products in the United States, Canada, and Mexico. Its European Operations are marketing coordinated wardrobe doors, frames, and interiors to established Western European markets. And its International Operations are focusing on marketing home decor products throughout the world (for more details, go online to: www.stanleyworks.com).

There's no question in my mind that this company can greatly improve its worldwide brand identity with a few simple brush strokes—and I'll get to that in a moment. Even more important, the Stanley name is capable of becoming a global powerhouse consumer brand on a scale that would send tremors through the towering Sears building in Chicago and the Ikea Group's headquarters in Sweden. Consider what this company's flagship brand (Stanley Tools) has going for it:

- It's a household word in America; many would say it's an American brand icon.
- It has a rich heritage; it's as much a part of Americana as Hershey's chocolate and Budweiser beer.
- It's all about quality products for home and professional use—durable products that offer good value for the price.
- It's known worldwide for precision craftsmanship.

It takes a brand vision to transcend the original product, and I can envision "The Stanley Store" dotting suburban landscapes in the United States and Europe and in hundreds of shopping malls in major countries. In addition to its current lineup of products, the array of new products that could be sold under the Stanley brand name is mind-boggling—furniture, kitchen cabinets, knives, cookware, flatware, bedding, linens, towels, glasses, candles, garden pots, and just about everything else for the home that exemplifies "The best in craftsmanship at a competitive price." Add to this crafts and art supplies for the entire family, ready-to-assemble furniture, and woodworking, masonry, and gardening kits all pre-packaged with the necessary Stanley branded tools to get the project done. This is all possible through private-label contracts with suppliers around the world to manufacture these products to the "design and quality" specifications of Stanley Works.

"The Stanley Store Concept" could be company-owned, or it could be based on a franchise system, with the franchisor being Stanley Works of America. Other cornerstones of this store concept could include the Stanley online and print catalog and the Stanley trademarks.

Undoubtedly, an international chain of Stanley retail stores would give the Stanley umbrella brand tremendous visibility with consumers worldwide. In addition, it would open doors for licensing agreements with other manufacturers who are looking to market their products under a powerhouse brand name. This could easily result in annual licensing fees in the tens and maybe hundreds of millions of dollars on a global basis—and, for the most part, all we're talking about here is monitoring the design and quality of products sold under the Stanley trademarks.

Now, let's consider what's needed to kick this brand up a zone on the Image Map to a "Status Label" appealing to both men and women.

First, professionals and do-it-yourselfers in construction, home improvement, woodworking, and agriculture refer to the company's umbrella brand as "Stanley Tools." But the word *tools* in the brand's name obviously limits the product range. The corporate name, Stanley Works, implies a workshop where metal is forged. So, it too conveys a limited product scope. The ideal name would be simple, easy to remember, distinctive, and capable of embracing a full range of craftsmanship home furnishings and garden products—from wrought iron front-door gates to Egyptian-cotton pillowcases. Well, the stand-alone Stanley name meets these criteria.

Second, the company's brand logo, featuring the name Stanley in bold sans serif capital letters in a horizontal bar reminiscent of an early American cabinetmaker's nameplate, is too rigid and unimaginative. The ideal brand logo would be visually captivating, contemporary, nonlimiting in product scope yet capable of embracing the brand's legacy of craftsmanship tools and hardware.

Third, the total packaging of the umbrella brand needs to convey a retail mentality, not a manufacturing mentality. The key to success for Stanley Works is making its umbrella brand more glamorous, inviting, yet believable in the minds of consumers—and that's the very brilliance behind Sears's advertising strategy today.

But the job's not over yet! A major marketing challenge facing Stanley Works and thousands of other companies like it that manufacture basic consumer and professional products is how to get buyers to identify with its brand and not the product's generic word. For example, most hosts would ask their invited guests, "Who wants a Coke, Seven-Up, Diet Pepsi, or Miller Lite?" Why is it that they don't say, "Who wants a cola, noncola, diet cola, or light beer?" Because, in their mind, the brand's name has replaced the product's generic description. Yet, when people need a hammer, they'll say, "Do you have a hammer?" Why is it that they don't say, "Do you have a Stanley?" Because in their mind, the brand's name is irrelevant—a hammer is a hammer.

If you want to catapult your company's brand into the realm of marketing stardom, you've got to encourage and educate consumers to remember your brand, and to say your brand's name to other people when they're referring to products that your company makes. There are ways to get people to mentally connect your brand's name with the product's generic word. Here's one such brand-building idea for Stanley Works. Label the handles of your hand tools with a statement like this: "It's not *just* a hammer—It's a Stanley," and then carry this theme through the entire product spectrum. Examples: "It's not *just* a wardrobe door—It's a Stanley"; "It's not *just* a wall mirror—It's a Stanley."

There's no question that the hottest vehicle for making your company's umbrella brand or flagship brands transcend the product is the company-owned brand store. Yet opening several megabrand stores on the scale of Nike Town or The Disney Store takes more than guts and determination. You'll need omnipowerful brands to endorse an almost endless array of products; you'll need to recruit people with experience and a proven track record in retail; and you'll need to be in a financial situation to make it all come to fruition—to mention just three things.

Now, the good news for thousands of manufacturers with no retail experience and limited financial resources is that they can launch their own online brand store at a cost of $10,000 or less. Here are some of the advantages to the online store: There are no costly storefront monthly rental payments; no physical store design to create, build, furnish, and maintain; and no middlemen and salespeople required. So, if you decide to go this inexpensive route and ship direct to the customer, you can pass some or all of the cost savings along to the customer and that translates into more value for your products in the buyer's mind. Many online stores are offering consumers 40 and 50 percent discounts on staple food items, electronics, and a host of other products bearing trustworthy brand names.

I predict that the franchise brand store concept will explode in unlikely places, and that the new franchisees will include management consulting, accounting, financial investment, and legal firms. I can't reveal much more because this subject will be addressed in my next book.

Building the Brand With the Internet

The Internet is a powerful medium with which to build the omnipowerful brand. And it will play an even greater role in the next century when an expected 120 million Americans will go online to do their shopping, trade stocks, seek entertainment, track new trends, manage their finances, find job opportunities, plan their family vacations, research dealers and brokers before making major purchases, and perform myriad other functions daily. To coin a new phrase, it will be "the mother of all electronic brand name libraries," easily eclipsing the 2.4 million U.S. registered brand marks filed with the federal trademark office in Arlington, Virginia.

Shopping on the Internet started in 1994. In the year ending 1998, it's estimated that $1 billion worth of goods and services will have been purchased online. Some are predicting that, by the year 2003, online shopping will soar to over $200 billion. Even the most conservative analysts put the number at $40 billion. True, commodity products like books, music CDs, airline tickets, packaged food, and computer software programs that consumers don't need to physically inspect will continue to be the big sales performers. But keep this thought in mind: If you buy a software program online, you can download it right off the Internet, and that saves a trip to the store.

You don't have to be a giant of industry to benefit from the Internet's awesome reach to tens of millions of companies and countless individuals worldwide. In fact, the Internet offers the greatest opportunities and cost savings to individual entrepreneurs and small to medium-size businesses. In marketing communications, it will eventually do to the commercial printing industry what the invention of the twist-off bottle cap did to the metal bottle cap and opener—make them almost obsolete. Now, think of the Internet as a prism with many sides. Here's one of them—the company's Web brochure (also called Web advertising).

To print, handle, and mail out 10,000 full-color, eight-page brochures covering a company's history, the brand-name products it makes, its services, why people should invest in it, and how to locate a dealer or sales representative could easily cost $30,000.

Now, for a cost of about $200, you can have your own domain (personalized Web address) on the Internet. And for a fee of about $50 per month you'll get 10 megs or enough Web space to upload an eight-page full-color Web brochure with photo and graphic images that can be accessed by anyone in the world with a computer or other device that's linked up to an Internet host server. And unlike a printed brochure, your Web brochure can be revised, with the information and graphics updated, at any time with no added cost.

Think about it: You no longer have to warehouse boxes of brochures, buy mailing envelopes, print mailing labels, purchase U.S. postage, print a covering letter, clip a business card onto the brochure, or pay a broker to coordinate the entire printing, handling, and mailing process. Now, here's the real kicker: Unless the product featured in your brochure is a hot news item like Tiger Woods, the young golfing sensation, 95 percent of the brochures you distribute will be tossed in the trash bin because of office paper clutter and another 4 percent will be returned or also disposed of because the addressee no longer works for the company. Based on real-life direct mail statistics, you'll be doing well if one-half of one percent of the brochures you mail are actually reviewed by your target audience. That means it cost you $600 to place just one of your brochures in the hands of someone who *might* have some influence on his company's decision to do business with your company. That one $600 brochure covers the cost of having your Web site on the Internet for one year.

The graphics, photo images, and text in a conventional printed brochure are also static by the limitations of offset lithography. Further, the reader's finger must do the walking to find the information she's looking for inside the soft-cover book. If the reader wants more information about a product or division mentioned in the printed matter, she has to make the effort to call or write the company, and that can be a time-consuming process. In contrast, your Web brochure can be animated, three-dimensional, interactive, and linked with other Web sites, thus expanding your Web brochure far beyond eight pages at no additional cost.

For example, if you access the General Motors Web site (www.gm.com), you'll find menu topics like Select a car, Locate a dealer, Choose a finance plan, Meet the family, Discover new terrain, Invest in GM. Point and click your PC mouse on "Select a car," and multiple windows open to reveal a menu of GM cars and trucks and magazine-like cover stories, including "Concept cars for the future," "Learn about the EV1," "America's first production electric car," and "Fashion's top designers take their creations on the road." You can open up any one of these magazines or select the GM car line you're interested in by pointing to the item and clicking.

If you open Saturn, you'll find a short profile of the car company that started out in a barn ten years ago. Want more electronic information on Saturn and its products? It's simple;

just point and click on the Saturn Website, and presto, you're inside Saturn's site (www.saturncars.com). Here you find a menu of topics like Now you can lease a Saturn, Talk to Saturn, Visit the Saturn Japan Web site, Submit your photo and see yourself on the World Wide Web, and much more. Plus, you can electronically enroll in Saturn's "Extended Family Database," sign up for the Saturn "Listserv," and request a current full-line product brochure.

Point and click on "Back" on the main tool bar and you're back to GM's home page to preview other topics. All the time you're surfing from one Web site to another, it's show time as colorful graphics and photo images come to life on the screen and animated illustrations point you in the right direction. And at any point you can print a copy of the image frame on your monitor; in fact, you can print out all the frames, staple them in page order, and end up with a printed document about GM, its divisions, its product lines, and where the auto giant is heading. Of course, if you're impressed with what you've seen and read on GM's Web site and the satellite sites linked to it, you may want to own GM stock; in that case, I suggest you point and click on "Invest in GM."

A Web brochure on the Internet is a must for start-up and small companies that advertise their brand-name products only in print media because of the high costs of producing and airing TV spots. If this fits your company's description, you can close your ad with "Visit our Web site (www.company-name.com) to preview our full line and to talk to us."

Before the advent of the technology that pioneered the Internet and the Web site, advertisers traditionally ended their print ads with an invitation to call an 800 number for more information. Now, with the Internet, there's a new way of looking at your company and it offers big advantages. For starters, target buyers who do visit your site and then talk to you by e-mail are more likely to buy your product because your Web brochure has provided them with the opportunity to see your products, your people, and your company in a television-like commercial. Can an 800 operator match that?

Another advantage of having such a Web site is to take care of all the tire kickers out there—people who have no intention of buying your product. They can visit your site and satisfy their curiosity and it's not costing you anything extra; your fixed monthly site fee covers frequent visitors and all new arrivals. The cost of tracking and following up on sales leads that never materialize into a sale can put a big dent in a small company's operating cash flow. God only knows how many start-ups and small businesses have gone out of business chasing after would-be buyers.

Companies in a service business like advertising and PR agencies, industrial, graphic, and packaging design houses, legal and accounting firms, and just about everyone else can include client information in click-on windows on their Web sites. Take my firm, for example. If you visit our Web site (www.frankdelano.com), you'll find some sixty examples of brand names created by the Delano firm for consumer products companies, automotive manufacturers, pharmaceutical and medical companies, financial institutions, electronic and photo-imaging companies, retail chains, and others. You can point and click on highlighted brand names and product photo images, and a window opens providing information about our clients and the products they have in the marketplace in addition to the product we named for them. Thus, we are using our Web site to help build awareness of our clients' brands; after all, without our clients, we'd have no business to run.

Here's another way the Internet can help to build your brand: promoting your site for free. Paid banner ads aren't the only way to attract potential buyers and users to your site. The key is to get listed—and listed right—on the hot links pages, finding and working the jumplists, getting media coverage for your Web site launches, enrolling in listservs, participating in newsgroups and topic forums, and using third parties and automated engines that provide site exposure. For example, you can e-mail your company's Web brochure from your PC to remote host computer engines like Yahoo that provide the vehicle to find information on the Internet. So, even if surfers don't know your Web address, they can still find your company's Web brochure on these computer engines, assuming that they ask for the product or business category you're listed under and you're listed with the engine they're using.

With all the fanfare about the World Wide Web, the "If you build it they will come" theory doesn't apply here. You have to get target buyers and users to visit your site. Once again, big-league advertisers have the edge in that their TV spots, which dominate the airwaves, remind consumers to visit their sites on the Web. And even if you don't remember their advertised Web address, the fact that they are household names makes it easy, even for beginning surfers, to find them using the URL. After all, logic tells you that if you're looking for Ford Motor Company's Web site, your first attempt would be http://www.ford.com. And your thinking would be right— this *is* Ford's Web address.

Let's say you have only a fraction of Ford's annual advertising budget to spend. How can you deliver potential customers to your site using the Internet? First start with the basic nuts and bolts of building awareness of your site. Find the best Web sites for your banner ads, measure and analyze ad response, create Web banners and buttons that pull and generate traffic for free through search engines and links lists. In fact, while I was writing this very paragraph I got a call from Jeff Rose, a trademark attorney based in Northern California. He wanted to know more about our process and our fee arrangement to develop a new corporate name for his high-tech client. I asked him how he had heard of my firm, and he said he was browsing Yahoo's search engine for naming firms when he spotted our listing. Having visited our site, he told me, he was impressed with our Web brochure and the names we've created.

Here are some other ideas for getting users to your site. Sponsor minisites linked to your global home page to target audiences who can build your brand; promote contests and prizes; and use interactive ads. Consider the emergence of audio and video ads and delivering ads to target buyers' desktops. Some companies are even paying surfers to view their site to build awareness with targeted audiences.

Because the success of any Web site is measured by how many visitors stop by, how long they stay, and whether they come back, many marketers are engaging animated and entertainment firms like Macromedia, which are known for their Shockwave technology games that are fun to play and addicting. But if your game is remembered and your product forgotten, you might as well start your site's home page with "Compliments of a friend." If you use a game or quiz, it should build on the brand's advertising theme. Maytag's Web site (www.maytag.com) is an excellent example. First they present their new Neptune washer with a statement that clearly positions the product as being a revolutionary way to gently get your clothes clean. Move forward and you'll quickly learn about the washer's benefits in four major areas: cleanability, capacity, care, and conservation. Whether your interest is in household or commercial laundry, you can click on any of six close-up product photo images that explain the breakthrough design and engineering features of the Neptune product.

The Maytag "Home of Dependability" site is reinforced by one of America's classic advertising figures, the veteran Maytag repairman, "The Loneliest Guy in Town." You can make a free copy of "Ol' Lonely's" favorite game—solitaire, of course.

Eveready's Web site (www.eveready.com) features a "Rabbit Test" to build on the famous Energizer pink bunny. But not before you learn that Eveready is soon introducing an Energizer on-battery tester for its AAA batteries, the fastest-growing cell size in the alkaline segment. This Energizer feature is already on three cell sizes, AA, C, and D. We also learn that *Popular Science* magazine named the new on-battery tester for Energizer brand batteries one of the best home technological innovations of the year.

Outside of the Internet, look for every opportunity possible to build awareness of your Web site. If you're a local, regional, or coast-to-coast moving and storage company, put your www.domainname.com on your vans in big type with a line like this: "Visit our Web site to meet our satisfied customers." If you make outdoor barbecue grills, as Weber does, put your Web address on the product's shipping cartons with a line like "Visit our Web site for tasty barbecue menus." In fact, if you go online and visit Weber's site (www.weberbbq.com), you'll find just that. The Weber site "gives new meaning to a menu-driven interface," according to *Ad Age*. Each month Weber serves up a barbecue menu, shopping list, tips, and even beer and wine recommendations. The site goes on to guide you through your choice of a grill with a quiz on the different types of grills Weber makes. And you can fill out a form to get information and tips and recipes sent via e-mail to you. If you're a retail bank or savings and loan, put your Web site address in big type on the windows of your branch offices with a line like "Visit our Web site to see how easy we've made it to get a home mortgage loan." Getting your Web address known by consumers is the way to build your brand. So, print it on shopping bags, billing envelopes and statements, and everything else that gets seen by the public. And don't forget to add a copy line that motivates consumers to visit your site.

Then there's another facet of the Internet to help support your product's integrity with customers. Many manufacturers are using the Internet to provide twenty-four-hour brand support and dialogue, equipment diagnostic testing, and downloading of software for buyers of their products. For example, when I was experiencing problems with the Resume Phase on my new IBM Aptiva PC, I discovered that the software in a microchip on the logic card that had been replaced by the dealer wasn't designed to work with Windows 95. Going on-line to IBM's Internet support service Web site, I was able to download the software I needed on a floppy disk. The problem was corrected after I installed the correct software.

Marketers who are serious about building the omnipowerful brand have to know everything about the brands they're competing against. This includes how each is positioned in the marketplace, its brand name, corporate and professional endorsements, logo and system graphics, packaging design, advertising campaign theme, brand spokesperson, point of purchase displays, and selling environments. It also includes knowing the competition's after-sales customer service and technical support backing their brand, special promotions, brand clubs for the family and kids, and any innovative brand-building ideas your competitors have found that you haven't.

How do you find such information fast and for free (or

almost for free)? It's simple, you just visit your competitor's Web site and any other sites linked to its home site. You may also learn about a new product your competitor has launched under a new brand name and other new products that are flowing through its development pipelines. Even if you don't find all the competitor's brand information you're looking for on the Web, comparing the graphic look, topics covered, and text navigation in your competitor's Web advertising with your own will tell you whether you need to go back to the cyberspace drawing board.

It's amazing how the dynamics of marketing can change with the arrival of breakthrough technology. Just a decade ago, the brand's TV advertising campaign was considered the silver bullet for moving the product out of the dealer's showroom. As more and more people turn to the Internet to shop for major products, the focus is gradually shifting to which company's Web advertising will get the consumer's attention first and hold it. Even the advertising industry's top-rated journal, *Advertising Age,* has a "CyberCritique of the week" in which new Web sites are reviewed by an editor for interactive media. As I have stated more than once in this book, conventional thinking on how to build the brand no longer works; it's a whole new world out there.

While the use of interactive media to build the brand is hot today, there are proven principles to follow to create great Web advertising. The home page has to grab the viewer's attention with compelling graphics. The headline, topics, and first paragraph of text have to draw the visitor in and pique his interest to dig in further, pointing and clicking to a topic he's interested in. Once he does dig in, he should find it easy to move around quickly, take what he needs, and get back to the home page or point and click to another topic he might want to browse.

The key is to make it simple yet entertaining. Think of a magazine format like that of *Cosmopolitan,* with jabbing headline punches announcing topics that address the questions asked most frequently by your target buyers. But remember, you're not writing a book here. Don't start off with a lengthy paragraph that goes beyond the screen's frame. If you feel compelled to tell a story, follow the writing style used by *The Wall Street Journal*; its articles almost always start with a one-sentence paragraph that pulls you into the story. Example: "Can you make money playing the presidential elections?"

Icons have become as popular on Web sites as the charm bracelet was to your mother or grandmother in the 1950s. Having too many of them will only distract from your message. I have visited some Web sites that are so riddled with decoy icons (that's an icon that you point and click on and nothing happens) that even Sherlock Holmes would find it a challenge to navigate around. If you use an icon, it should serve a functional purpose like moving you around the Web site with greater ease. The beauty of cyberspace is the speed at which you can travel to visit Web sites around the world and get information on almost any topic. Your message should communicate fast, too.

The Internet today is far from being a marketer's panacea, and it may not be the right medium for everyone. But then again, it's still in its infancy. As I speak, revolutionary concepts in marketing the brand via cyberspace are emerging almost weekly. For example, the U.S. Postal Service is currently testing the plausibility of purchasing CyberStamps. This means that in the near future you may be able to use your PC to purchase postage electronically and receive a bar code via e-mail. When your PC speaks to your printer, the bar code—with the right postage—is automatically printed on the envelopes running through your printer.

Here's one more facet of the Internet I haven't yet mentioned: You have a global audience out there that's just a mouse click away from buying your products and services. Now, that's a *powerbat* idea every company can afford to have in its marketing dugout.

The Revival of a Vanishing Medium

Yes, I have stated that an electronic medium like Web sites on the Internet offers great opportunities to build brand image power. But as the world of brand communications moves more and more into the realm of cyberspace, there's something to be said in favor of reviving the personalized executive monarch letterhead and envelope as a means of communicating the brand's value, character, integrity, equities, and growth opportunities in new and expanding markets to targeted audiences like customers, new venture capitalists, investors, Wall Street's shakers and movers, and the business press.

True, the time it takes the U.S. Postal Service or private carriers like FedEx and UPS to deliver a letter or package to the addressee is no match for e-mail. But then, can e-mail as a split-second communications medium compete with the personalized executive monarch letterhead when it comes to making an indelible brand impression on the reader's mind? And what gets more attention today, e-mail or postal mail?

Most of the executives I talked with in researching this subject told me that they simply forget to check for e-mail messages on a daily basis. One in particular said it would be wonderful if she could simply turn on her desktop computer's media console and find a message on the monitor's screen that she had e-mail, and then a simple point and click on a menu bar would instantly open up a window of her electronic mail. Until technology makes this happen, however, one has to first go online to check for daily e-mail messages. What I discovered was that many businesspeople tend to wait until they have a need to go online to see if they have e-mail. When they do and then find twenty or thirty electronic messages titled G. Anthony, M. Marcus, S. Stevens, and so forth, they say it's a real time-consuming chore to figure out which e-mail requires an immediate response and which are from companies that want to sell their wares to them or from nonprofit organizations looking for donations.

These same executives said that no day goes by when they don't preview their mail delivered by a U.S. postal carrier. Unlike viewing e-mail, a simple glance at each envelope in the stack reveals by its size, graphics, color, paper quality, and printed message what's important to open, what can wait, what should be tossed in the waste bin unopened, what are personal bills, and so forth.

Unquestionably, when businesspeople see an executive

monarch envelope bearing a prestigious stationery house watermark with the sender's name printed, engraved, or embossed on the envelope's square flap, it gets priority attention. Why? The very look and feel of this medium tells them that the information inside must be important, timely, and to the point. I say "to the point" because the smaller format size of a monarch letterhead, as compared with the larger American standard letterhead, invariably dictates the need for verbal brevity by the writer.

There is a magic about this medium that can't be quantified in words, but the people I interviewed said a handwritten note or printed message on a premium-quality executive monarch letterhead seems to have an intrinsic and historical value to it, especially if it's signed by a business executive or professional with celebrity status or by some up-and-coming entrepreneur who holds the promise of someday being a prominent figure in his field. They agreed that this could not be said if the same message was received in the form of a facsimile, mailgram, or e-mail printout.

They admitted to having no problem disposing of correspondence written on standard company letterheads that they have received over the years. Yet, when they come across letters in their files written on personalized monarch stationery, they can't seem to let go of them. Who knows, in the next century the holders of personalized executive monarch letters signed by William Gates, Steven Jobs, Warren Buffett, Donald Trump, Carl Icahn, Baron Hilton, Malcolm Forbes, or Thomas J. Watson, Jr., among a host of other noted business celebrities of the twentieth century, might just gain thousands of dollars auctioning them at Christie's. Well, I recently learned that many people in the business world share these sentiments.

Last year, my firm designed and conducted a quantitative market survey of business executives and administrative assistants across the country to determine which direct communication medium is most effective in building a brand's image. The findings confirmed the brand-building effectiveness that the personalized executive monarch letterhead has over other mediums such as the facsimile, e-mail, mailgram, standard letterhead, and FedEx Priority Overnight.

What I found striking was that the facsimile received the lowest rating score for brand-building effectiveness among the respondents surveyed, and it appears to indicate that this medium no longer has communication impact. To be more specific, our research revealed that a staggering 98 percent of fax transmissions to corporate decision makers go unread if the message is unsolicited. In fact, a number of executives said that their companies have stopped publishing fax numbers on all printed materials owing to the deluge of unwanted solicitations received on a daily basis. Keep in mind that the paper cost to receive these unsolicited letters is borne by the receiver, not the sender.

In contrast to this, 100 percent of the respondents said that they promptly open and read all letters that arrive in the form of a personalized executive monarch envelope. These same executives said that they almost always write a short note back to the sender thanking him for his thoughtful letter and saying that it will be kept on file for future consideration. Now, that finding speaks clearly to the communications power of this medium.

The second-highest rating score for communication effectiveness went to the FedEx Priority Overnight, which came as no surprise considering the $13 to $15 average delivery charge for use of this medium. The standard letterhead was ranked third in the survey. E-mail received a below-average score for sales effectiveness for the reasons I've noted earlier. Mailgrams were rated only slightly above facsimiles because they're a dead giveaway to an unwanted solicitation, according to most of the respondents. They also happen to be the choice of medium for scam operators who swindle countless millions of dollars from consumers each year with ploys like "You've won a new car, but before you can pick it up, you have to remit a money order for the sales tax."

Hands down, our research showed that the most effective direct communication medium with which to build your brand's image with target audiences is the personalized executive monarch letterhead and envelope. But like any medium, it's the message that counts. We also learned what style of written letter works, and what doesn't work.

Here's what works:

- *A letter coming from the chairman, CEO, president, CFO, group vice president, or executive vice president.* This makes the reader feel that he's speaking with one of the company's highest-ranking executives.

- *Dating the letter beginning with the day followed by the month and year (3 June 1998) to convey an international customer base.*

- *Starting off with a statement that draws attention to the sense and substance of your reason for writing.* This should be followed by a brand message that's informative, timely, and brief—no more than four short paragraphs. Select a 12-point classic type font like Times Roman or Helvetica. Be generous with your margins and the space below the signature line. The overall appearance of the finished letter should look inviting and easy to digest.

- *Making it believable.* The letter should sound as if *you* wrote it, not someone else. To accomplish this, write in a way that comes naturally to you, using words and phrases that come readily to mind. Keep the language simple, using strong and accurate nouns and verbs, and hold back on the adjectives and adverbs. This is the style that works best for this medium.

- *Speaking to the brand's essence, uniqueness, or spirit.* For example, if "breakthrough technology" is the brand's hallmark, make this point in the first paragraph and back up your statement with facts.

- *Explaining why doing business with your company is a better alternative than doing so with the competition.* If you have a product that's superior to the competition's, simply tell your story without bragging.

- *Making a pledge that your company is committed to the brand's integrity and after-sale service support and giving the reader examples.*

- *In closing, inviting a dialogue with the reader and providing the vehicle for making it easy for her to do so.* For instance, you might invite her to attend a special event to see the brand's product line up close. Say that you'll be there and look forward to meeting her.

- *Using a converted (not a stock) monarch envelope with a substantial square flap and engraving your company's name and address on that flap.*

- *Selecting a signature postal stamp that fits the image of the brand's theme in the written message.* You'd be surprised by how many assistants to the president and CEO will notice this special touch as they prioritize his or her mail.

Here's what doesn't work:

- *Not dating the letter.* This is a dead giveaway that it's a commercial mass mailing. The reader will instantly see through the seeming sincerity of the words and phrases directed to him or his company's needs.

- *Starting off with a hard-hitting selling proposition that never seems to stop.* Remember, the very look and feel of this medium dictate a statesman-like, soft-sell approach. Going against the natural grain of this medium will destroy the object of your letter, which is to build the brand's image in the reader's mind.

- *Overstating anything about the brand.* Whether it relates to the product's value, character, integrity, service support, or potential growth, overstatement is one of the most common faults in direct communication mediums. A single overstatement or a single carefree superlative will put the reader on guard, and has the power to diminish the entire message because the reader loses confidence in your judgment.

- *A breezy, garrulous style of writing.* Too often the writer imagines that everything that pops into his head will be of interest to the reader. Don't blow wind when you're writing business prose. Place yourself in the background and think about what the reader wants to hear about your brand.

- *Printed text and your signature appearing on the letter's reverse side to save the expense of a second sheet.* This is clear evidence of a commercial mass mailing.

- *Underlining text, highlighting text in yellow, emphasizing key points with bullets, and printing the sender's signature in light blue.* These are obvious giveaways that the letter was written, printed, and packaged by a direct mail marketing firm. If the writing is solid and good, you don't need these devices. You can reveal the brand's message without appearing anything less than a top-level corporate executive.

- *Adding a P.S. below the signature line reading "Take advantage of our low finance rate by completing the attached form."* Suddenly, the letter's message is no longer statesmanlike, personal, and believable.

- *Adding a printed statement on the face of the envelope.* Messages like "An Exclusive Invitation for Professionals," "7.9% APR—No Annual Fee," or "The New Standard of Excellence" are more than likely to send your well-crafted brand-building letter into the waste bin unopened because it looks like direct mail advertising.

- *Stamping the envelope with metered postage or printing "Presorted First-Class Mail U.S. Postage Paid XYZ Company."* This is clear proof that thousands of businesspeople are receiving the same message.

Out of context, the engraved personalized executive monarch letterhead and envelope printed on premium watermarked paper sounds like just another sales gimmick. Actually, long before fax machines and computer modems came into the picture, this medium was considered *the proper format* for corporate executives to use to express their ideas, business propositions, and new product launches in writing to other business decision makers. With the advent of the company controller and his legions of number crunchers, this medium, which can run four times the cost of do-it-yourself laser-jet–printed stationery, has all but vanished from corporate America. As a result, the engravers of fine-quality business stationery have dwindled down to a fraction of what they numbered in the 1970s. But why is it that many successful marketers who are masters at building the omnipowerful brand remain faithful to this medium, and don't flinch at the paper cost and printing bill?

It's because they know that when you add up the sales numbers, you get more brand image power with this medium than with the less expensive alternatives; it's that simple. And I predict a revival of this medium as we enter the next dimension in power brand marketing.

Forming Marriages With Other Omnipowerful Brands

Thirty years ago, would an ad agency's senior account executive dare to recommend to a major client that it feature another company's brand name in its commercials? Had he done so, chances are that the executive would have been fired or removed from the account by his own agency, or that the agency itself would have risked losing the account because of its executive's incomprehensible suggestion.

How the world of brand marketing has changed! Today, if a company's management is not exploring opportunities to form marriages with other companies' omnipowerful brands, many would question its ability to manage and build the company's flagship brands.

Linking your company's brand with other manufacturers' successful brands makes your brand look more attractive to consumers and that can translate into higher sales of your products. This is not a new trend that's here today and will be gone tomorrow. It happens to be one of the smartest marketing strategies for the twenty-first century, and it's already paying big dividends to those companies that have adopted it. Consider these examples: TV spots for Infiniti cars remind target buyers of these vehicles that Bose brand-name speakers are standard equipment. Computer PC makers like IBM and Gateway 2000 promote the latest Intel Pentium processor and Microsoft's Windows 95 software as product features. The voice-